The New Rural Economy

Change, Dynamism and Government Policy

The New Rural Economy

Change, Dynamism and Government Policy

BERKELEY HILL

WITH CONTRIBUTIONS FROM DAVID CAMPBELL,
CHRIS CARTER, BARRY GAMBLE, JOHN HIBBS,
BOB LEE, JOHN MEADOWCROFT, JULIAN MORRIS,
RICHARD D. NORTH, SÉAN RICKARD,
AILEEN STOCKDALE AND PAUL WITHRINGTON

FOREWORD BY GEOFFREY HOWE

The Institute of Economic Affairs

First published in Great Britain in 2005 by
The Institute of Economic Affairs
2 Lord North Street
Westminster
London SW1P 3LB
in association with Profile Books Ltd

The mission of the Institute of Economic Affairs is to improve public understanding of
the fundamental institutions of a free society, with particular reference to the role of
markets in solving economic and social problems.

A CIP catalogue record for this book is available from the British Library.

ISBN 0 255 36546 2

Many IEA publications are translated into languages other than English or are reprinted.
Permission to translate or to reprint should be sought from the Director General at the
address above.

Typeset in Stone by MacGuru Ltd
info@macguru.org.uk
Printed and bound in Great Britain by Hobbs the Printers

CONTENTS

PART III: FARMING, FORESTRY AND THE ENVIRONMENT

THE AUTHORS

David Campbell is Professor and Head of the Department of Law, University of Durham. Bob Lee is a Professor in the Cardiff Law School and Co-director of the Centre for Business Relationships, Accountability, Sustainability and Society (BRASS), a research centre based at Cardiff University which receives its principal funding from the UK Economic and Social Research Council. Campbell and Lee's work on the 2001 foot-and-mouth epidemic has been supported by BRASS.

Chris Carter is Head of Parliamentary Affairs at the British Property Federation, a trade association that represents the UK commercial property industry. Prior to joining the BPF, Chris worked as a Research Associate for the Adam Smith Institute, a free market think tank. Chris is a graduate of the Universities of London and Cambridge. He writes here in a personal capacity – the views expressed in his chapter do not necessarily represent those of the BPF or its members.

Barry T. Gamble is chairman of fountains plc, the environmental services company. The forestry division handles the management of some 750,000 acres of UK softwood plantations and US Appalachian hardwood timberlands. The properties are managed for a range of private, institutional, public and trust owners based in the UK, the USA, Europe and the Middle and Far East.

John Hibbs, who has written widely on passenger transport, started his career in the rural bus industry and has remained in touch ever since. His book *A Country Busman* (DTS Publishing, 2003) tells what it was like running buses in God's own county (Suffolk) in the 1950s. Some things don't change.

Berkeley Hill was Professor of Policy Analysis at Wye College and, following merger, at Imperial College London. Since October 2005 he has been emeritus professor. His research has focused on economic statistics for agriculture and the evaluation of rural development. He has been consultant to the OECD, Eurostat, the European Commission, the United Nations and the UK government.

Lord Howe of Aberavon (Sir Geoffrey Howe) was a Conservative MP from 1964 to 1992, Chancellor of the Exchequer from 1979 to 1983, Foreign Secretary from 1983 to 1989, Deputy Prime Minister and Leader of the House of Commons from 1989 to 1990.

John Meadowcroft is Deputy Editorial Director of the Institute of Economic Affairs and Lecturer in Parliament and Politics on the Hansard Scholars' Programme at the London School of Economics and Political Science. His first book, *The Ethics of the Market*, will be published by Palgrave in December 2005.

Julian Morris is Executive Director of International Policy Network, a London-based think tank, and a Visiting Professor at the University of Buckingham. The author or editor of many papers and books, including *Environment and Health: Myths and Realities* (2004) and *Sustainable Development* (2002), Julian previously ran the IEA's Environment and Technology Programme and is a member of its Academic Advisory Council.

Richard D. North is the IEA's media fellow. The Social Affairs Unit published his *Rich Is Beautiful: A Very Personal Defence of Mass Affluence* in April 2005 and will be publishing his *Mr Blair's Messiah Politics: Or what happened when Bambi tried to save the world* in the autumn of 2005. Richard has written on 'green' issues, including farming, for most of the broadsheets over the past 30 years, especially for the *Independent* and the *Sunday Times* (1986–92).

Séan Rickard is Senior Lecturer in Business Management at Cranfield University School of Management. Séan studied economics at the London School of Economics and Birkbeck College, London, and has an MBA from Cranfield School of Management. Prior to joining Cranfield in 1994 he worked as a business economist, and from 1987 was Chief Economist with the National Farmers' Union.

Dr Aileen Stockdale is a Senior Lecturer in the Department of Geography and Environment at Aberdeen University. She has written extensively on the impacts of in- and out-migration flows on rural areas of the United Kingdom. She also contributes to the rural surveying and planning syllabus at Aberdeen University.

Paul Withrington has a BSc in Civil Engineering and an MSc

in Transport Planning. He is a C.Eng (Chartered Engineer) – a Member of the Institution of Civil Engineers (MICE). Currently he directs Transport-Watch – dedicated to making the best use of transport land in the interests of the community as a whole. Most of that work is directed to exposing the railway myth that has led the government to subsidise rail for the past 50 years.

FOREWORD

Politics and economics often find themselves at odds with each other. Countryside policy is no exception. At one level, we are constantly reminded that agricultural employment in most developed economies occupies no more than 2 or 3 per cent of the workforce – and, supposedly, is of no electoral significance. Yet the largest mass demonstration in recent British history was staged by the Countryside Alliance.

My years of political partnership with Margaret Thatcher demonstrate the same point. At no less than eleven World Economic Summits (and about twice as many EU Council meetings) we argued for the curtailment and reform of the CAP – and for action against Japanese and American agricultural protectionism. Yet once back home, after making weekend political tours around Britain, when we met again in Downing Street on Monday mornings, Margaret would often exclaim: 'We must do something for our farmers, Geoffrey!'

So clearly, although these essays are focused largely on British symptoms, the authors are in truth addressing themselves to a pandemic disease.

It was high on the agenda at the first of many OECD ministerial meetings that I attended, in 1973. Since those days the degree of infection has been measured by reference to the percentage PSE – Producer Support Estimate. That assesses the proportion of gross farm receipts which is derived from support measures of *all* kinds (tariffs, subsidies or whatever).

For the OECD countries as a group that figure has fallen since 1986–88 from 37 per cent to 31 per cent in 2001–03. Put the other way around, this means that farm receipts (in the OECD countries) were on average 60 per cent higher than they would have been if entirely generated in world markets without any support. By 2001–03 this figure had fallen to 45 per cent.

The level of support, of course, varies widely. For Australia and New Zealand it is under 10 per cent, in the USA about 25 per cent, in the EU almost 40 per cent, with dramatically higher figures for Japan (60 per cent), Iceland, Norway and Switzerland (70 per cent).

In so far as there has been a reduction in these figures in recent decades, this appears to have been largely achieved by (persistently reluctant) partnerships – the EU for many and the WTO for some major outsiders.

The worst 'offenders' appear to be those (excepting Australia and New Zealand) who have been going it alone: notably, in Europe, those who are free to indulge in competitive (and not Common) agricultural policies. But I must not be tempted to stray outside the essentially national framework of this thought-provoking work.

One thing is absolutely clear. If any real headway is to be made in tackling the problems of 'countryside policy', whether in response to international pressure or not, that must depend upon the will and wisdom of national leaders, working within their own societies. These essays will offer them important guidance along that track.

GEOFFREY HOWE

ACKNOWLEDGEMENTS

The IEA would like to acknowledge the generous support of the Esmée Fairbairn Foundation for this publication.

As in all IEA publications, the views expressed herein are those of the individual authors and not those of the Institute (which has no corporate view), its managing trustees, Academic Advisory Council or senior staff.

SUMMARY

- Billions of pounds of taxpayers' money are spent each year on government policies directed specifically at the problems of the countryside, yet it is not clear what constitutes the countryside nor that rural areas experience problems distinct from those also experienced by urban and suburban areas.
- Over 84 per cent of government spending on rural areas is in support of farming, yet agriculture accounts for only 3 per cent of rural employment. Tourism is a much more significant contributor to the rural economy, but the needs of the tourist industry are often put second to those of agriculture – as was the case with government policy in response to the 2001 foot-and-mouth crisis.
- Subsidies to agriculture maintain uneconomic activity contra to the government's aim of creating a 'sustainable' rural economy. Low-income farmers are deemed worthy of special financial support, but low-income workers in other occupations do not receive similar help.
- The National Farmers' Union and other agricultural pressure groups continue to exert a strong influence on government policy, which may in part explain why the farming sector continues to enjoy such privileged treatment.
- In-migration of commuters, second-home owners and

retirees brings positive economic benefits to rural areas which are not always appreciated. Policies aimed at preventing such migration, such as 'locals-only' housing policies, are likely to be ineffective and counter-productive.

- There has been an increased politicisation of the land-use planning system in the countryside as planning is increasingly seen as a means of achieving a set of political objectives determined by central government.
- Car owners in rural areas are hard hit by car tax, vehicle excise duty, VAT and fuel tax, while local authorities and central government subsidise public transport, notably school buses and the Community Rail network. The social and economic case for such subsidies is not proven. A strong case exists for ending the enormous government subsidies presently paid to rural railways.
- The present role of the Forestry Commission, as adviser to government on forestry policy, industry regulator, loss-making and market-dominant commercial operator and, probably, timber seller of last resort, should be reformed. Its multiple roles may conflict and there is a strong case for allowing the forestry industry to develop and self-regulate free from state direction.
- The decline of nuisance law in favour of the use of the law of negligence since the late eighteenth century may be a strong causal factor in the poor levels of environmental conservation in the countryside. A return to nuisance law may provide a means of dealing with pollution and polluters in the courts without the need for government intervention.
- A number of government departments and public agencies presently implement a wide variety of countryside policies.

The case for many of these interventions is at best unproven and at worst non-existent. Very often supposed market failures are 'remedied' by far more damaging government failures. Better outcomes may be achieved if government simply did nothing.

TABLES, FIGURES AND BOXES

The New Rural Economy

Change, Dynamism and Government Policy

1 INTRODUCTION
John Meadowcroft

In the summer of 2005 Devon County Council advertised for a new chief executive by creating a fake road sign that read 'Welcome to Devon: home of rural deprivation, a low income economy, property inflation, an ageing population and your next challenge'. The negative depiction of Devon implied by the fake road sign caused controversy in the county which found its way into the national press.[1] It also articulated what many policy-makers believe to be a set of problems specific to the country-side. Rural areas are believed to be characterised by social and economic 'exclusion' and a predominance of low-wage jobs, rising house prices that prevent people from purchasing houses where they want to live, and a large elderly population that may put particular pressures on service deliverers. At the root of these problems is believed to be the decline of the agricultural sector of the economy, which has exacerbated the difficulties faced by rural areas. The problems of the countryside are widely believed to necessitate widespread government intervention.

Certainly there is no shortage of bodies with policy-making responsibility for the countryside. The Department for Environment, Farming and Rural Affairs (Defra), the Department for Transport, the Office of the Deputy Prime Minister, the Coun-

---

1   For example, *Daily Mail*, 15 July 2005, p. 31.

tryside Agency, English Nature, the Rural Development Service, Regional Development Agencies, Regional Assemblies and a host of local authorities all have responsibility for spending billions of pounds of public money in the pursuit of government policies directed specifically at the problems of the countryside. This monograph assesses the policies pursued by these myriad institutions. It assesses whether the goals of present countryside policy are desirable and achievable.

This introduction is followed by an overview of present countryside policy by Professor Berkeley Hill of Imperial College London which constitutes the first of three main sections of this monograph. Professor Hill identifies a number of reasons why present policy may not be the most appropriate response to the many challenges facing rural areas.

First, the evidence base for the government's countryside policy may be questioned. It is not clear, for example, what constitutes 'the countryside', nor that the problems of rural areas are distinct from those of urban areas. What constitutes the 'countryside' or the 'rural' may be defined by policy-makers in order to justify a specific government intervention: the large amount of public money spent on farming (over 84 per cent of government spending directed at rural areas), for example, may be justified by defining rural areas in terms of traditional agricultural employment, when in reality agriculture accounts for only 3 per cent of rural employment.

While it may be believed that agricultural employment (and its decline) make the countryside unique, the reality is that tourism employs more people in rural areas than farming. Furthermore, many of those who live in the countryside work in suburban or urban areas or are employed in occupations similar to their suburban and urban counterparts. There is also evidence that people in rural areas want the same quality of life improvements as those living in urban and suburban localities: countryside dwellers and their urban counterparts all want to see better healthcare and high-quality education, be able to afford better housing and have access to improved transport. Throughout the rural–urban continuum people share the same concerns about their jobs, quality of life, health, their children's education, the housing market and the cost of transport.

It is possible to question whether the UK needs a countryside policy at all. Indeed, as Hill notes, it is particularly odd that low-income farmers are believed to merit financial support from the government whereas other poor people are not: why are low-income farmers privileged in a way that low-income taxi drivers and low-income sales clerks are not? The reason is probably twofold. First, agriculture has occupied a special place in the public consciousness since the time when Britain was largely dependent on home-grown produce. Second, the agricultural lobby has historically been powerful throughout western Europe and has consequently been successful in securing special privileges and rents from government. Low-income taxi drivers and sales clerks, however, do not have a similar place in the public consciousness, nor similarly organised and influential organisations to lobby on their behalf.

Government assistance to agriculture is also an example of a subsidy to an inefficient industry. When government uses subsidies to support economic activity that would not be maintained by market mechanisms the result is a net loss of welfare. Agricultural activity that is not economically viable is supported by taxpayers, removing the incentive to diversify into new methods or new products. The cost to the economy is not only the money required to support such activity, but the opportunity cost of economically viable enterprises that are not undertaken because resources have been used elsewhere. Even those in receipt of subsidies may lose out in the long term if they do not have the time or motivation to explore the possibilities of more lucrative endeavours. Subsidies to agriculture may therefore be a cause of poverty.

Indeed, as Hill points out, while agricultural subsidies are often justified in terms of 'sustainability', in reality, 'If the aim is really a competitive and sustainable agriculture, then the market should be allowed to operate in such a way that there is pressure on the uncompetitive and unsustainable units to exit.' By their very nature, subsidies allow unsustainable activity to continue, whereas the operation of market mechanisms would apply pressure on people to engage only in sustainable activity, thus creating a healthy and robust agricultural sector just as market forces have done in those sectors of the economy where they have been allowed to operate.

As with all areas of public policy, demonstrating that markets do not work perfectly, or that the functioning of markets sometimes produces difficult consequences for some people, does not necessarily justify government intervention. The costs of market failure (in terms of 'imperfect' outcomes) have to be weighed against the costs of government failure (also in terms of 'imperfect' outcomes). A countryside policy may not be the best solution to the problems of the countryside if the costs of intervention exceed the costs of doing nothing. Hence, Hill argues that government may have a role to play in the rural economy, but it is clear that such a role has to be informed by a more robust evidential base that takes into account the costs as well as the benefits of intervention.

After Professor Hill's overview of countryside policy, the second and third sections of this book consist of ten shorter chapters that examine particular aspects of rural economics and countryside policy. The second section looks at the related questions of migration, planning and transport. In Chapter 3, Dr Aileen Stockdale of Aberdeen University examines the impact of in-migration on the rural economy. Stockdale provides evidence to show that in-migration offers rural areas positive economic benefits. Whereas statutory bodies charged with bringing about the economic regeneration of rural areas may perceive in-migration of commuters, second-home owners and retirees as part of the problem that faces rural areas, Stockdale's evidence suggests that in-migration may be an important driver of economic regeneration. Incomers spend a large proportion of their income locally and self-employed migrants in particular tend to generate new employment for long-standing residents. In this respect, it would appear that the absence of government intervention – allowing the benefits of in-migration to work through the rural economy rather than seeking to manage in-migration – may be important in bringing about rural regeneration.

Chapter 4 examines the spread of 'locals-only' housing policies: restrictions imposed by local authorities on who can buy or own properties in particular localities with the aim of ensuring that those on relatively low incomes can afford to buy properties in particular locations. These policies have a particular salience in the countryside, where it is widely believed that the in-migration of those seeking to take advantage of the amenities offered by rural areas pushes prices beyond the reach of the sons and daughters of long-standing residents. This chapter shows that such policies are unlikely to achieve their stated objectives because they do not address the mismatch between supply and demand in the housing market that lies at the heart of house price inflation. Moreover, they are at odds with the fundamental principle of a free society that scarce resources should be allocated by the choices of consumers and producers in the marketplace rather than by political authority.

'Locals-only' housing policies are an attempt to deal with some of the problems caused by the UK's land-use planning regulations, which limit the supply of new houses. In Chapter 5, Chris Carter shows how the nationalisation of planning through an enhanced role for central government agencies and a lesser role for local authorities is leading to the politicisation of planning in the UK: land-use planning is being used to achieve a set of political objectives determined by central government. A prime example is the government's Communities Plan, in which the government plans to spend £22 billion over the next decade developing new homes and transport infrastructure in special earmarked 'growth areas'.

Like 'locals-only' housing policies, such an approach replaces the idea that the price mechanism should determine the nature, scope and size of development with the notion that central government should plan growth down to the number of new houses needed many years into the future and the exact road space required to service such planned development. Carter exposes the pathologies inherent in such an approach and proposes a dynamic alternative based upon genuine localism which involves granting real autonomy to local authorities so that different localities may offer competing models of planning regulation, leading to a process of creative discovery similar to that which takes place in private markets.

One area where the countryside and the rural economy may

face a distinct problem is in transport policy. Whereas urban and suburban areas face the problem of traffic congestion and over-crowded public transport, rural areas may be faced with the high cost or absence of both public and private transport. Rural road users, for example, may be hit particularly hard by petrol tax if they travel relatively long distances each day. In the sixth chapter, John Hibbs, Emeritus Professor of Transport Policy at the University of Central England, charts the decline of bus and rail use in rural areas in the last century and the concomitant rise of the private car.

The rise of the car in the countryside also coincided with the decline of traditional agricultural employment; as rural residents had to travel farther in search of employment the car became close to a necessity. As a result, the key transport problem for people in the countryside today is the cost of motoring. This is determined by two factors: taxation and the cost of fuel. While government has little control over the cost of fuel, the combination of car tax, vehicle excise duty and VAT, in addition to the fuel tax, produces revenue for HM Treasury far in excess of government expenditure on roads. Hence, in 1999 road users paid a surplus of some £26 billion to government, over and above the total road expenditure. By contrast, local authorities presently subsidise a wide range of public transport in rural areas, including school buses and bus services to deep rural villages. Hibbs identifies a situation where one group of rural residents subsidises another. This is not necessarily a redistribution from the rich to the poor, but may be a subsidy from low-income workers who must use a car to travel to their place of work to middle-class parents who have the cost of their children's journey to and from school subsidised.

Hibbs proposes two solutions to the problems facing countryside transport. First, the lowest level of local authorities should take the lead in bringing together private providers of transport and local residents to see how their different needs and preferences can be dovetailed – this could be done at parish council level. Such a process may alert private bus companies, for example, to hitherto untapped demand for their services. Second, a regime of road pricing in place of the present triple tax levy faced by road users may reflect the real cost of motoring in different localities and thereby encourage and allow a greater number of rural dwellers to use private cars – it has been estimated that a fully efficient system of road pricing may increase rural car use by 25 per cent as a result of substantially reduced costs.

A more iconoclastic view of rural transport is provided by Paul Withrington of Transport-Watch in Chapter 7. Withrington argues that the present functions of heavily subsidised rural railways could be provided more efficiently by converting those railways into roads. At present the Community Rail network carries a tiny number of passengers and its contribution to the rural economy is minuscule – almost certainly smaller than the £300 million annual subsidy that the network receives. The subsidy to rural railways persists because of the widespread acceptance – among the public, politicians and officials – of a number of faulty assumptions about the social, economic and environmental benefits of such railways. Withrington argues that we presently face a choice as to whether rural railways are converted into economically viable roads, abandoned to wildlife or continue to be subsidised as 'full-sized, fully working transport museums'. Certainly, without enormous government subsidies rural railways could not be considered viable.

The third and final section of this book examines the questions of farming, forestry and the rural environment. In Chapter 8, David Campbell of Durham University and Bob Lee of Cardiff Law School highlight the importance of government failure as a cause of the 2001 foot-and-mouth epidemic. Campbell and Lee argue that the Ministry of Agriculture, Farming and Fisheries' (MAFF) assumption of responsibility for disease control among livestock and its payment of generous compensation for animals slaughtered as a result of disease control measures made livestock practices conducive to the spread of contagious diseases like foot-and-mouth endemic because producers had no incentive to take preventive measures. Indeed, given the compensation figures paid to some livestock dealers as a result of the foot-and-mouth epidemic, the policies of MAFF may have acted as an incentive to encourage the spread of disease.

Given the relative importance of tourism and agriculture to the rural (and UK) economy, it also has to be asked why the tourist industry was jeopardised at the expense of the livestock industry? Campbell and Lee conclude that a similar outbreak and its tragic consequences for the rural economy and animal welfare can only be avoided in the future if Defra takes steps that require the livestock industry to internalise the cost of disease control by treating it as a standard business expense rather than a public good to be provided by government.

Richard D. North argues that the present level of government subsidies to farmers makes farming the last state-run production industry. In Chapter 9 of this collection, North emphasises the significance of UK membership of the EU and the Common Agricultural Policy in allowing the enormous subsidies to farmers to continue for so long; had subsidies been implemented by Westminster, they would probably have been abandoned decades

31

ago. As the case for EU (and other) agricultural subsidies has evaporated in the face of an increasingly efficient global market in food, however, it is now proposed by the EU that farmers are paid to do things other than farm, such as provide environmental benefits. A viable future for UK farming, North envisages, will involve market-driven diversification that may mean some land returning to wildlife and the development of other land, along with the further development of organic, free-range and factory farming to cater to specific niches in the food market. What should be abandoned, North argues, is the role of government in picking winners in terms of what goods are produced and who produces them.

In Chapter 10 Séan Rickard of Cranfield School of Management examines the role of the UK farming lobby in ensuring that for decades agricultural interests have dominated countryside policy and farming has remained a protected and subsidised industry. Rickard describes how although the National Farmers' Union of England and Wales remains the most powerful of the countryside interest groups, its influence has waned in recent years as the status of farming has changed and more militant and broad-based countryside lobby groups – notably the Countryside Alliance – have become an important focus for rural interests. Rickard warns, however, that it is a mistake to believe that the NFU has lost all its power. On the contrary, the importance of agriculture to the government's countryside policy described in detail by Hill is evidence of the enduring power of the farming lobby.

The importance of agriculture and the farming lobby to UK countryside policy means that many activities crucial to the rural economy are frequently marginalised in policy debates. UK forestry is one such example. In Chapter 11, Barry Gamble,

Chairman of fountains plc, a private company providing forest management on some 750,000 acres in Scotland, England, Wales and the USA, argues that the countryside has been poorly served by the Forestry Commission – the government department responsible for the management of the UK's forests and woodlands. Gamble argues that the fundamental problem facing UK forestry is the multiple and conflicting roles performed by the Forestry Commission as adviser to government on forestry policy, industry regulator, loss-making and market-dominant commercial operator and, probably, timber seller of last resort. Whereas forestry in other countries has developed into an important asset that is part of many investment portfolios, Gamble shows how attempts to manage and direct UK timber markets and forestry policy by the Forestry Commission in its various guises have hampered similar developments in the UK.

The solution, according to Gamble, is to change the remit of the Forestry Commission. Its regulatory role should be passed to an independent regulator, although such external regulation need be minimal as the industry has demonstrated that it is well capable of self-regulation with many private forests currently managed to independently recognised sustainability criteria. Present public sector forests should then be privatised or – if such land is particularly environmentally sensitive – placed into public trusts following the model of the National Forests of the Midlands. In this way, UK forestry may follow the lead of other countries and be transformed from a struggling sector into a dynamic and investment-rich industry.

The final chapter in the collection, by Julian Morris of the International Policy Network, examines the attainment of environmental protection. This has taken on renewed significance for the countryside in the light of the government's recent emphasis on environmental conservation and sustainability as central objectives of countryside policy.

Morris argues that problems of pollution and environmental degradation may be linked to the decline of nuisance law in favour of the law of negligence since the late eighteenth century. Whereas nuisance law provided individuals with an effective means of satisfying their subjective preferences for environmental outcomes by taking legal action against those who had infringed their right to the enjoyment of their property – irrespective of what precautions had been taken to prevent nuisance – the law of negligence instead requires the identification of specific failures by polluters, implying a statutory framework of what reasonable actions should be taken to prevent pollution: the fact that a factory pours noxious smoke into the air is no basis for legal action unless it can be shown that some negligence has taken place. Morris's chapter points to a way forward in which the problems of environmental pollution and conservation may be addressed via the courts without the need for government intervention that brings with it the inherent danger that the policy process will be captured by producer or political interests to the detriment of the natural environment.

This collection provides an incisive analysis of many aspects of countryside policy and makes a number of positive proposals for change. Very often, positive changes are more likely to be achieved by a reduction in government's role rather than the creation of new legislation necessitating new interventions. But the analysis of Berkeley Hill shows, at the very least, that interventions in the marketplace very often do not follow sound economic principles. If the government wishes to see a truly sustainable rural economy, then it must cease to subsidise practices that are not economically viable. While the farming lobby, politicians and civil servants may still believe that the rural economy must be based upon plough-shares and livestock, if market forces were allowed to operate we might discover that a successful and dynamic countryside is more likely to be founded upon bed-and-breakfast hotels and fibre-optic networks.

PART I

OVERVIEW OF COUNTRYSIDE POLICY

2 A POLICY FOR COUNTRYSIDE PROBLEMS
Berkeley Hill

Introduction

The countryside impinges on most of us in one way or another. Quite what is 'countryside' is open to dispute, though this does not stop people thinking they know what it means and having an opinion on how it has been changing. Only about a fifth of England's population lives in rural areas – though the percentage varies widely according to how this term is interpreted. But a much higher proportion of us have an interest in the countryside, as we travel through it, use it for recreation or see it as part of the national fabric that helps make England as we know it. Surveys of public attitudes show that access to nature and the countryside is believed to be a fundamental part of our quality of life (Countryside Agency, 2004a).

The character of the countryside is the result of a complex interaction of factors, and huge differences exist between types of rural area. Some characteristics can be considered as making positive contributions to the well-being of the people who live there or who visit, such as a general lack of noise, pleasant views, etc. Many of these attributes are in the nature of 'public goods'. Others may be negative, such as the additional private costs (or poor availability) of accessing basic services and the need for private transport that often accompany remoteness. The bundles of positives and negatives vary according to the geographic location and affect different groups in various ways. The environmental benefits from low-intensity farming in the uplands are different from those resulting from farming on peri-urban fringes. The social and economic problems of people living in the countryside sandwiched between major conurbations in the South-East of England are very different from those of the remoter parts of Northumberland. Even in a single county such as Kent there can be wide disparity; the people living on Romney Marsh face very different conditions from those that exist on the outskirts of Maidstone. And the perception of whether a problem exists will depend on who you are. Splendid rural isolation may be sought after by affluent refugees from busy cities but pose a problem to a small business trying to expand its market or to households without private transport.

Many types of stakeholders – individuals, interest groups, voluntary organisations (some of whose rural roots go back a long way) and the public sector – are concerned with changes that have been taking place in countryside characteristics, alterations brought about by economic, technical, social and other drivers (Roberts, 2002). What is remarkable is the explosion since the late 1990s in the central government's awareness of rural issues and the growth of official activity in assessing their importance and development. In England the Countryside Agency,[1] created in 1999, has a special responsibility to advise government on rural issues. Since the publication of the Rural White Paper, *Our coun-*

---

1   The Countryside Agency was created in 1999 to bring together the different dimensions of the countryside – economic, environmental, community and enjoyment – though its roots can be traced back to the Development Commission of 1909 and the National Parks Commission of 1949 (later the Countryside Commission).

tryside: the future – a fair deal for rural England, in 2000 (DETR/ MAFF, 2000) much work has been done on developing indicators by which change can be monitored. The formation of the Department for Environment, Food and Rural Affairs in 2001 has greatly sharpened the focus of responsibility for the countryside. The review by Lord Haskins in 2003 on the way in which policies for rural England are delivered (Haskins, 2003) has resulted in a recently announced (2004) reorganisation of the agencies concerned.

As will become evident later, policy for the countryside has two main strands of concern. The first is the economic and social conditions of *people who live in areas that can be labelled as rural*. The second is with the *natural resources found there*, particularly the ways they are used and the environmental implications that affect people wherever they live, to a greater or lesser extent. For example, the appearance of the countryside is something of importance to people who live in urban and in rural areas, though perhaps in different ways.

The need for a special policy for the economic and social aspects of the countryside is open to question. A common assumption is that such problems are particularly acute in rural areas. Agriculture, the prime land user, is well known to be in sectoral decline (especially in the numbers of people it engages) as the result of the treadmill of technological change and fairly static demand for farm commodities. Agricultural adjustment is also commonly hampered by the relative difficulty encountered by its mainly self-employed workforce in finding alternative employment, and an inflexible land market. Distances from urban centres and low population densities bring with them economic handicaps. A simplistic approach to the countryside might therefore expect rural areas to suffer from declining populations, generally low incomes (but wide disparities), high unemployment and poor business opportunities, high costs of many basic necessities, poor and declining services, inadequate housing conditions, and poor human and social capital. This is the view that seems to dominate the thinking at EU level on rural development policy, as revealed in documents outlining proposals for the period 2007–13 (European Commission, 2004).

In reality the picture for England is rather different and far more complex, as will be demonstrated below. According to many indicators now becoming available, the quality of life for people living in the English countryside on average compares rather well with conditions in many urban areas, particularly inner cities. Where economic and social problems occur (access to health and social care, housing for relatively low-income groups, employment opportunities, etc.), they are rarely unique to the countryside, though there are some rural twists (such as the mixing of low-income households with more affluent ones, whereas in towns they tend more to be clustered). There is huge variation in the problems, both between locations and between groups of people.

Perhaps the most pervasive myth, and one that still dominates the rationale behind much current policy intervention, is that agriculture is the driver of the rural economy. The main vehicle of public spending directed at rural areas is support given to agriculture. As the principal land users, agriculture and forestry clearly have an impact on the environment and landscape. Their direct economic role in most rural areas, however, is of far less importance. Taking a long view, market mechanisms have proved successful in switching resources out of these primary industries and achieving a diversity of job and income opportunities, so that the composition of economic activities found in the countryside is remarkably similar to that of the national economy. Supporting agriculture fails to address the most serious economic and social problems of rural areas. Though agricultural policies have a role in achieving environmental goals, it is likely that the crucial link is with the farming system rather than the number of farmers, pointing towards a more efficient means of delivery.

This paper argues for taking a radical approach to the countryside and policies aimed at it. It poses a number of fundamental questions. What are the real (in contrast to the assumed) problems in the countryside – economic, social, environmental, etc. – and what are their underlying causes? Which problems are the products of market failure, for which a case might be made for government intervention in principle? Which of these are economic in nature, in the sense that they imply a loss in GNP that government intervention might avoid? Can markets be made to work better? Which market failures involve environmental or social services that are essentially public goods? Beyond market failure, which problems are issues of equity (for which a rationale for public action may exist, but one that should be differentiated from that for market failure)? Which problems are attributable to government failure, in the sense that past public choices have worsened or created problems?

If a problem exists, is a policy to address it justified? Is intervention efficient, in the sense that there is likely be a net gain to society from using resources in this way? The cost of intervention may compare unfavourably with the benefits overall, in which case the economically efficient policy may be to do nothing at all. For environmental and societal problems, is it feasible to base the arguments on the valuations attached to environmental and social externalities, and what is the quality of these estimates? Where the rationale for policy action is based on equity, is it possible to achieve the desired outcome in a less resource-demanding way?

On a more applied level, what policies are in place in England to tackle problems, and are they appropriate? Have we learned from past experience of what works and what does not? Why devote the large majority of public resources flowing into countryside policies to supporting farmers when they do not form the core of poverty in rural areas and resources directed this way do not deliver solutions to the other countryside problems in ways that appear to be remotely efficient? As a complement (perhaps an alternative) to government support to agriculture, which, in the main, cushions farmers against the economic pressures to change, how can the impediments to adjustment be eased while, at the same time, safeguarding the characteristics of the countryside that society wishes to protect? Few of these questions can be addressed in depth here, but at least raising them may lead to more consideration being given to the present policy for the countryside.

This paper is divided into sections that reflect the conventional approach of policy analysis. They boil down into two main issues: first, what are the problems that are believed to exist and which form the basis for policy for the countryside (the evidence base), and, second, what policies do we have, do they work, and what might be done better? The sections are as follows:

- What we mean by countryside – an outline of the rural–urban continuum and the close inter-mixing of town and country in much of England.
- What are the economic, social and environmental problems associated with rural areas?

- Rural statistics – evidence for policy action – information and statistics about the countryside that can act as the evidence base.
- Agriculture and rural areas.
- Policy for rural areas – what we have in place.
- Sustainability and policy.
- The shape of a more efficient and less inhibiting policy for rural areas.

What we mean by countryside – the rural–urban continuum

The 'countryside' is a popular and politically powerful notion, but an imprecise one. The potential for confusion when looking at countryside problems and policies can be reduced if the meaning of 'rural' can be sharpened up, because 'rural areas' and the 'countryside' are often used interchangeably. Awareness of the lack of a clear rural/non-rural division is by no means new, with the close inter-mixing of countryside and development seen in much of southern England causing comment from at least the mid-nineteenth century (see Box 1). More recently, evidence assembled in *The State of the Countryside 2001* (Countryside Agency, 2001) demonstrated that a range of concepts of what constitutes rural have been defined and made operational by public institutions, and a study of UK rurality (SERRL et al., 2001a) listed some ten different approaches in use. Attempts to define the rural areas in the UK have varied from the largely intuitive through those based on single indicators (land use, population density and so on) to more formal statistical definitions incorporating multi-variate analysis of indices deemed to indicate rurality (the various

Box 1 **Anthony Trollope – *The Three Clerks* (1858)**
'It is very difficult nowadays to say where the suburbs of London come to an end, and where the country begins. The railways, instead of enabling Londoners to live in the country, have turned the country into a city. London will assume the shape of a great starfish. The old town, extending from Poplar to Hammersmith, will be the nucleus, and the various railway lines will be the projecting rays. There are still, however, some few nooks within reach which have not been be-villaed ...'

Quoted by Dot Wordsworth, *Spectator*, 23 October 2004

approaches are reviewed in Hodge and Whitby (1986), SERRL et al. (2001a)).

A crucial point is that the most appropriate definition of rural will depend on the aspect of the social, economic and natural part of the environment the particular policy wishes to influence. For example, if the problem is lack of access to hospital services resulting from remoteness, then it is the distance of the place of residence (or time needed to cover the distance) which is the important issue, not the nature of the land use surrounding the household dwelling. Conversely, if the problem concerns change in the environment, such as the presence of wildlife, then agriculture is important and the definition of rural must incorporate how land is used; whether the people who live in the area have access to services is not relevant. A substantial danger exists that a definition of rural, created for and appropriate to one purpose, may be

Box 2 **Purposes for defining 'rural'**

In the *Preliminary Draft Final Report* (SERRL, 2001a) five broad types of purpose were identified, though the distinctions are not absolute (they have been rearranged from the original).

- *For the statutory allocation of resources.* The only clear example of this in England is the 'Right to Buy' provisions of the legislation in relation to rural housing, requiring clear definition.
- *For the more or less direct targeting of resources.* An example is the two-stage process by which a broad allocation is made centrally to qualifying rural districts, then local authorities select appropriate areas within their jurisdiction; Rural Bus Grant and Rural Business Rate Relief are examples of this process.
- *In the construction of various 'headline indicators'.* Those in the Rural White Paper are likely to require appropriate definitions of 'rural'.
- *For constructing urban/rural statistical descriptions.* This frequently used and important application requires consistency between the geographical units used to create the urban *and* rural definitions and administrative areas (including wards and parishes).
- *For analytical purposes.* These include the locating of survey points within urban areas and the population banding of urban areas for sample survey and data-reporting purposes.

hijacked and used in situations where it is manifestly a misfit.[2] Box 2 shows some of the different purposes in the public sector.

Despite that principle, there is an understandable drive for an agreed general-purpose definition of what constitutes a rural area, something that can be shared across government departments, other public bodies and commentators on countryside change. The lack of a common approach has been a particular handicap when attempting to bring together statistics produced by different bodies. Deciding what is rural is especially difficult when there is a close inter-mixing of urban development and more traditional rural land uses. For example, in southern England the countryside is often fragmented by substantial urban areas, suggesting that the classification into rural and non-rural has to be based on quite small geographical areas. In contrast, large areas of Wales are similar in terms of land use, population density and with no large settlements occurring in them, so that 'rural Wales' can be taken as an entire group of nine large unitary authorities.

In March 2001 the then Department for Transport, Local Government and the Regions (DTLR) commissioned from a consortium of universities a study of urban and rural definitions used for policy purposes. This review (SERRL et al., 2001a) concluded that the three sets of criteria commonly used to assess rurality (land cover, population characteristics and social/economic organisations) had become, in a sense, increasingly out of step. It commented that 'when it comes to defining and delineating urban and rural areas for policy (i.e. practical) purposes, [the fact that the terms 'urban' and 'rural' have become increasingly indistinct] means that no single solution is likely to meet

---

2   An example of misuse apparently occurred in the case of rural housing (NAC Rural Trust, 1987).

Table 1 **Population of England: percentage by type of urban and rural area, 2001**

Type of area (analysed at Output Area level)	% of population
Urban	81
Less sparse rural town	9
Less sparse rural village	7
Less sparse – dispersed rural settlements	3
Sparse rural area	1

Source: Countryside Agency (2004a: Annex 1)
Figures do not add up to 100 because of rounding-up

more than a "fair proportion" of the range of policy requirements'. The review nevertheless considered that 'an approach
involving the combination of data could appear more "definitive" and be more easily defended among a wide range of people'.
Follow-up research has come up with a classification system based
on hectare grid squares that takes into account settlement form (a
range from urban through village to dispersed dwellings), sparsity
or remoteness (based on the number of households surrounding
the hectare square) and function (numbers and types of commercial addresses). These hectare squares can be assembled upwards
to classify Census Output Areas, electoral wards, local authority
districts, etc. (see Annex 1 of Countryside Agency, 2004a). Table
1 shows that, using this new approach, about four out of five of
England's population live in urban areas, the remaining one fifth
being found in rural areas of various types, though even there
most live in towns and villages. Only 4 per cent of the population
live in what might be described as open countryside.

This classification system, validated in 2004, is too new to
have become widely used, and for the purpose of this paper
reliance must be placed on older approaches. Statistics quoted

49

here mainly come from classifications of (a) district and unitary authorities into urban and rural, further divided into remote rural areas and accessible rural areas, as used by the Countryside Agency in its *State of the Countryside* reports;[3] (b) electoral wards into rural or urban, again used by the Countryside Agency; (c) urban settlements (defined variously from population thresholds of 3,000 upwards, but with 10,000 a common figure), rural areas being those outside these settlements. Substantial differences in coverage (area and population) arise from using the different definitions. Though the existing evidence base comprises a diverse collection of these (and other) approaches, it is adequate to paint the broad picture needed here.

What are the particular economic, social and environmental problems associated with rural areas?
Government perceptions of problems

Concern with the problems of rural areas and with ways of assessing them has long existed but rose to prominence in the late 1990s. The Rural White Paper of 2000 (DETR/MAFF, 2000) was an important milestone, with its list of headline indicators (see Annex 1). The Countryside Agency has developed a very similar set of indicators. At the strategic level, a good indication of what are currently perceived as the problems of rural areas can be taken from the government's document *Rural Strategy 2004* (Defra, 2004a). This gives three priorities for rural policy

3   On this basis, some 28.5 per cent of England's population lived in rural districts. This system was based on economic, social and demographic structures but came up with some distinctly odd results (Folkestone, on the Kent south coast, with excellent road and rail communications and with France easily reached by ferry or Channel tunnel, found itself classified as remote rural)

that reflect government perceptions of underlying problems relating to living conditions in the countryside and threats to the natural environment:

- economic and social regeneration – supporting enterprise across rural England, but targeting greater resources at areas of greatest need;
- social justice for all – tackling rural social exclusion wherever it occurs and providing fair access to services and opportunities for all rural people;
- enhancing the value of our countryside – protecting the natural environment for this and future generations.

These three correspond to the top level of a hierarchy of objectives, and below them appears the detailed sub-objectives by which they are to be delivered. Details are spelled out in the Countryside Agency's 2004 *Review of Countryside Issues in England* (Countryside Agency, 2004b). This gathers concerns into four broad groups (i) people and communities – including demographic issues and community vibrancy; (ii) services and lifestyle – including geographical availability of services, access to affordable housing, rural mobility and emerging social issues such as rural childcare; (iii) environment and recreation – including changes in countryside character, biodiversity and sustainable land management; and (iv) economy and enterprise – including business health, the prosperity of market towns, and income and employment.

The annual *State of the Countryside* reports running from 1999 (an important input to the 2004 *Review*) have contained an evolving list of themes, which are further broken down into sub-themes for

Table 2 Themes contained in the Countryside Agency's *State of the Countryside 2004*

Countryside Agency theme	*Comments*
Population characteristics	Net population loss is a key indicator of other problems, but is not typical of England, where numbers have been rising in all but the most remote areas. Imbalance among age groups may both reflect existing economic and social problems and be the cause of them. Only in the 16–24 age band have there been recent net losses.
Public concern for the countryside	Analysis of surveys of perceptions of quality of life reflect some 22 different factors, many of which correspond with the themes listed here.
Community vibrancy	Seen as a positive feature of rural life, but indicators are usually indirect, such as the presence of a local pub, village hall, shop, primary school or church.
Health and special needs	Health standards are generally good, but there are physical, institutional and cultural barriers to rural residents accessing health services
Rural crime	Freedom from crime is seen as a major determinant of the quality of life. Crime levels are low but there was a rise in violent crime in 2002/03.
Geographical availability of services	Rural areas, being dispersed or containing only small settlements, present problems, especially for people without private transport
Access to affordable housing	A shared problem with urban areas, and reflecting income distributions
Education and training	Human capital is an important factor in securing employment and in being able to adjust to changing economic conditions and job markets

Countryside Agency theme	*Comments*
Rural childcare	Seen as both a basic service and as a way of enabling parents (especially mothers) to be economically active
Rural mobility	A particular problem for low-income and elderly residents
Traffic effects	Need to travel may be greater in the countryside. More traffic can lead to environmental deterioration.
Changes in countryside character and countryside quality	Important to many aspects of the countryside and difficult to quantify, but the Countryside Agency has developed indicators of change
Natural resources	The general picture in terms of air, water and soil quality is now reasonably good
Biodiversity	Habitat loss is still a problem in some areas
Sustainable land management	Land use by agriculture is likely to become less intense under most farming systems
How people use the countryside	The countryside is increasingly regarded as a resource for people living in urban areas
Business health	Non-agricultural businesses are the main sources of employment and income and of their growth
Market towns prosperity	Market towns embedded in the countryside are important centres of economic activity and of services to people in the surrounding areas
Employment characteristics	The role of agriculture is small and in decline. A broad industrial base and entrepreneurial activity are helpful to economic growth
Income levels and distribution	Income levels are key to solving many other problems, with the incidence of low incomes important to deprivation.
ICT in rural areas	Seen as critical to business life and of facilitating access to basic services and information

which indicators are suggested. The most recent set of headline themes is given in Table 2, to which comments have been added.

Public perceptions of problems

An important indicator of where the public sees problems occurring in rural areas (in contrast with the perceptions of politicians, administrators or academics) comes from a recent MORI national omnibus survey that classifies settlements of up to 10,000 as rural (MORI, 2004, quoted in Countryside Agency, 2004b). The emphasis is on the socio-economic aspects of countryside issues, corresponding to the first two of the priorities in the government's *Rural Strategy 2004*. When asked about what made their local area a 'good place to live', among a list of twenty-two factors the great majority of people (70 per cent) indicated freedom from crime to be a top priority, something that applied equally to people from rural and urban areas (Table 2). Similar high values were attributed to the presence of health services (61 per cent rural/59 per cent urban) and affordable housing (63/58 per cent). Beyond these three, another eight characteristics were scored highly, a broad mix of socio-economic and environmental features, including transport, job prospects, clean streets and unpolluted surroundings, and access to nature and the countryside (something that was rated only slightly lower by people in urban areas than in rural ones, 54/48 per cent).

Light is thrown on the perceived problems in local areas by questions about the aspects of quality of life that people felt most needed improvement. The most wanted features, shared equally by rural and urban communities, were facilities for teenagers, affordable housing, public transport and highway maintenance, with job prospects following after these issues. Compared with urban residents, rural residents saw more need to improve public transport (a particular problem in the more rural of the areas) and facilities for shopping and leisure. In contrast, rural residents saw a smaller need in terms of crime reduction, education service, a range of social features that reflected the general vibrant nature of rural communities (such as community activities and events), and environmental features that are associated with lower-density living (less need for easing traffic congestion or improving access to the countryside).

The conclusion is that the perceptions by residents of rural areas of what determines the quality of their lives are demonstrably similar to those of the population in general. A person uprooted from an urban area, particularly a city centre, to a rural one might find themselves in a strange physical environment, with land use dominated by agriculture and forestry and not many people about, but they would be familiar with many of the social and economic problems (lack of access to affordable housing or to healthcare, etc.). Some of these difficulties might appear rather less severe in the countryside than in a big town.

Many of the socio-economic problems perceived by rural residents are linked with remoteness or low population density. An important issue is freedom to choose. For those with resources to provide themselves with means of transport, the poor access may be no more than an inconvenience, and a price worth paying for the other benefits of living in the countryside. For the less well off, or those in other ways trapped in rural isolation, the problems associated with remoteness may assume far more importance. A gulf may thus exist between those who chose to live in the countryside, perhaps moving to do so, and rural residents of longer standing whose opportunities may be constrained.

Table 3 **Things in the local area that most need improving, %**

Improvement needed	Settlement size					All England
	<3k	3–10k	All rural	>250k	All urban	
Low level of crime	14	17	16	37	34	31
Health services	9	10	10	14	15	14
Affordable decent housing	30	27	27	26	27	27
Education services	7	5	6	14	13	11
Public transport	42	30	34	21	25	27
Clean streets	13	11	11	32	20	25
Shopping facilities	17	19	18	10	12	13
Job prospects	21	17	18	20	21	21
Access to nature and the countryside	3	1	2	7	6	5
Low level of pollution	8	4	6	14	13	11
Good neighbours	3	2	3	8	6	6
Open spaces and parks	5	2	3	12	11	10
Low level of traffic congestion	12	15	14	23	24	22
Facilities for young children	17	15	16	23	22	21
Activities and facilities for teenagers	35	35	36	31	35	34
Wage levels	11	12	12	9	13	13
Road safety	14	12	12	17	14	14
Sports and leisure facilities	23	14	17	14	13	14
Community activities and events	8	5	4	12	12	11
Road/pavement maintenance	36	27	30	27	29	29
Access to culture	4	5	3	8	7	7
Race relations	6	4	5	11	8	8
Other/don't know	1/3	0/8	1/3	2/5	3/6	1/4

Note: Multiple answers do not sum to 100%

Source: MORI, 2004, quoted in Countryside Agency (2004a)

But concern with the quality of life of people resident in rural areas is only part of rural policy. The countryside also represents a major environmental resource for society in general. Another group of problems, corresponding with the third priority in the government's *Rural Strategy 2004*, is to do with environmental issues or, to quote the words of the 1999 Rural White Paper, 'To conserve and enhance rural landscapes and the diversity and abundance of wildlife (including the habitats on which it depends).' These appear among the themes of the Countryside Agency's *State of the Countryside* as changes in countryside character and countryside quality, natural resources, biodiversity and sustainable land management. A methodology to trace changes in countryside character, which is multi-factoral in nature, has been developed, generating results that indicate that over the course of the 1990s about a quarter of the English landscape underwent changes that were marked, implying that further change may be a problem. The ten-yearly Countryside Survey now undertaken by Defra suggests that, while the rate of change in important features such as field boundaries during the 1990s was much slower than previously, some changes were still of concern (such as losses of stone walls in Lincolnshire and the Yorkshire Wolds, where they are essential parts of the traditional scene). Land losses from agriculture are now small, though the location of the transfers are of concern. In the late 1990s the greatest net losses were in counties surrounding the larger conurbations and the main axes between them, notably the London-to-Birmingham corridor. Thus while problems remain, according to the Countryside Agency the last five years have seen a more widespread recognition among land managers and developers that it is important to preserve a range of important countryside features (Countryside Agency, 2004b).

The pictures presented in these official reports on the quality of natural resources (air, water, soils) and biodiversity seem to be quite good (ibid.), largely thanks to steps already taken, and do not contain urgent warnings about mounting problems for which further actions are needed. Some difficulties remain, however; for example, though the English lowlands are no longer losing habitats overall, the distribution of habitats remains fragmented and their quality is declining.

Rural statistics – evidence for policy action

Until recently the evidence base for many of the problems of rural areas has been remarkably ad hoc and, in places, flimsy. When the Countryside Agency started to report on the *State of the Country-side* (in 1999; the 2004 edition is its sixth) it faced a major task of assembling evidence from disparate sources using a variety of basic units. This weakness in the statistics necessitated the Agency (primarily a user of data) taking the initiative as a collector of data on some issues (such as availability of services). When in June 2001 the Ministry of Agriculture, Fisheries and Food (MAFF) evolved into the Department for Environment, Food and Rural Affairs, the state of statistics on its new enlarged responsibilities was very lopsided. A wealth of agricultural statistics existed, built up from over a hundred years of experience in measuring produc-tion, prices, land use, the farm labour force, etc., but relatively little was available about the social and economic conditions in rural areas.

The necessity for a 'data infrastructure' to assist with rural issues and policy is now widely recognised and the deficit in England is in the process of being rectified. Following a report on how Defra could meet its new information needs (Hill, 2002), a system of small area statistics is being developed. This uses as a model the Neighbourhood Statistics of the Office for National Statistics, a system that brings many data-sets together using Census Output Areas (COAs) – smaller than electoral wards – as the linking unit. Neighbourhood Statistics now labels each COA as rural or otherwise. A major advantage of taking the disaggregated approach is that it makes the assembly of economic and social statistics on rural areas potentially much more flexible, as the basic statistical units (COAs) can be selected in ways to meet the problem in hand (standard rural definition, or special alternatives such as distance from a conurbation). For the exploration of problems that need a large geographical area, because either the countryside feature of interest (such as predominant farming types) demands this or because the available data are insufficient to support analysis of small areas, COAs can be combined.

Basing rural statistics on COAs does not provide a complete solution. For examining some rural problems it is necessary to have very detailed information; if, for example, a characteristic of poverty in the countryside is that poor people are inter-mixed in the community with affluent people, then even COA-level data may hide the low-income cases in an average household income that appears quite satisfactory. A much smaller unit needs to be taken to explore the distributional issue, perhaps even the individual household. Data on individuals and on households (demographic details collected by censuses, household survey data, tax returns, etc.) are increasingly coded to their addresses, which can, or could, be linked to COAs.

In parallel with this new system for rural socio-economic statistics, Defra has brought together environmental data-sets and the various designations of areas and sites using geographical coding, both in an internal system and by being one of the public sector partners that set up the Multi-Agency Geographic Information for the Countryside (MAGIC) system in 2002. The various statistical initiatives, including the ten-yearly Countryside Survey and the annual survey on land use changes, mean that, in the view of the Countryside Agency, we are in a good position to be able to track changes in the character of the English countryside over time (Countryside Agency, 2004b).

But evidence is not confined to statistics. There is a major role for specialist studies of the nature of the many changes taking place, drivers and appropriate indicators, linkages to the rest of the economy, etc. A glance at the websites of Defra, the Countryside Agency and other bodies with rural interests reveals that since about 2000 there has been a flood of research reports and evaluation exercises. Defra has announced the establishment of a Rural Evidence Research Centre as part of its *Rural Strategy 2004*.

To sum up, the evidence base (both statistics and other research), though not yet entirely satisfactory, is rapidly improving.

Patterns in statistics for rural areas

The information coming from statistics and studies is beginning to show that the actual problems are rather different from past assumptions. Contrary to common preconceptions, the people who live in the countryside are not particularly disadvantaged. Rather, according to most indicators, rural areas do rather well; where problems exist, they are more to do with distributions.

A general point is that, in many ways, rural areas are no longer unique. The occupational composition of rural areas in England is very similar to that of the country as a whole, as is demonstrated by evidence from the latest Population Census (Table 4), which classifies respondents into the industry of their main activity. Only in the relatively greater importance of agriculture (and fishing) in rural areas – hardly a surprise – does there appear to be much difference, and even in rural areas they account for less than 3 per cent of employment (including self-employment). Other and somewhat earlier sources had put the figure higher, though the upper estimates were only about 7 per cent. In both rural and urban areas the public sector, finance and manufacturing were the main employers.

This similarity of economic structure has been known for some time, though it has received public endorsement in two documents from the centre of government which took an overview of rural policy and its objectives: these were the report to the Prime Minister by the Cabinet Office, *Rural Economies*, in 1999 and *Sharing the Nation's Prosperity: Economic, social and environmental conditions in the countryside*, in 2000. Importantly, these also contained broad descriptions of the living conditions of rural England which, at this high level, dispelled the myth of general rural disadvantage and economic and social decline. Subsequently the information was updated by the Countryside Agency in its annual *State of the Countryside* reports (indeed, there is textual evidence of substantial overlap between the Countryside Agency's early reports and these Cabinet Office papers).

There is room only for a brief summary of the main features emerging from the statistics. Though there are methodological differences between data sources, these are unlikely to make much difference to the general patterns.

Table 4 **Employment by sector, 2002 (%)**

	Urban	Rural
Agriculture and fishing	0.3	2.6
Energy and water	0.6	0.8
Manufacturing	12.7	15.4
Construction	4.2	5.1
Distribution, hotels and restaurants	24.1	26.7
Transport and communications	6.5	5.2
Banking, finance and insurance, etc.	21.9	15.1
Public administration, education and health	24.3	24.1
Other services	5.3	5.1
All	100.0	100.0

Source: ONS Census 2001 given in Countryside Agency (2004)

Population change and demographics: Rather than suffering falling numbers, most rural areas are net gainers of population; only the most remote areas recorded losses in the last two decades. Migration is the main cause of change in population. Censuses are, of course, snapshots, and there will have been both inflows and outflows even where the totals remain stable. The migration from urban to rural areas is now four times that of the drift in England from north to south. In terms of the age composition, rural areas are again quite similar to non-rural ones (see Figure 1). True, there are relatively smaller numbers of people in their late teens and early twenties, and the sixteen-to-twenty-four age group is the only one in which more people are migrating to urban districts than to rural ones, but there are many factors to explain this, including life-cycle events such as going away to higher education and training, the facilities for which are usually in urban areas.

Incomes and employment: The average gross weekly earnings in rural areas are less than in urban areas (£431 as compared with

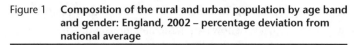

Figure 1   **Composition of the rural and urban population by age band and gender: England, 2002 – percentage deviation from national average**

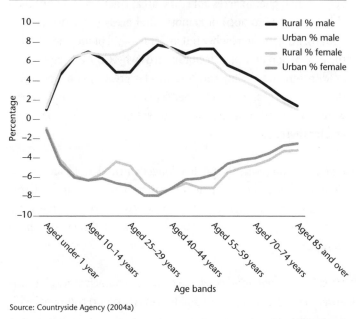

Source: Countryside Agency (2004a)

£473 in 2003), with remote rural districts (£404) doing less well than accessible rural ones (£453). The largest rural/urban differences were seen in the South-East (14 per cent) and the South-West (12 per cent), and the smallest in the North-East (1 per cent). Earnings, however, are not the same as household income. Overall the distribution of household income in rural areas was similar to that in urban ones, and at national level there was no difference between the proportions in income poverty (23 per cent of households with incomes less than 60 per cent of the median, which was £22,400). Another basis of calculation (using local authority districts) shows that median household incomes in 2002 were higher in accessible rural areas (median £28,200) than either urban (£26,000) or remote rural areas (£23,800) (Defra, 2004b). Looking at a higher but arbitrary level of income, in 2003 the proportion of urban electoral wards where the average household income was below £20,000 was far greater, at 9.5 per cent, than among rural wards (2.0 per cent). Levels of unemployment were lower in rural areas, and the recent growth in jobs has been greater there.

Health and longevity: People live longer in rural areas and are in generally better health than those in urban areas. In part this helps explain the age profile mentioned above. Suicide rates among men, however, are higher in rural areas, though they have come down.

Homelessness and social benefits: The level of homelessness is much lower in rural areas (38 households in every 10,000 compared with 68 urban households) though it has risen substantially in recent years and there may be under-reporting. The provision of social housing is less in rural areas (13 per cent of the stock compared with 22 per cent in urban districts), even though earnings levels are lower. The proportion of rural households receiving key out-of-work benefits is less than half that of urban households.

Crime: The incidence of crime and the fear of crime are much lower in rural areas, though there has been a recent statistically significant increase in violent crime.

Access to key services: Contrary to the popular perception, a high proportion of rural residents live close to key service outlets. Data from the Countryside Agency for 2002 show that over 90 per cent live within 2 kilometres of a primary school or post office, and increasing the radius to 4 kilometres gives 91 per cent for a cash point, 87 per cent for a doctor's surgery, 79 per cent for a supermarket, 76 per cent for a bank or building society and 76 per cent for a secondary school, many of these services being located in small towns rather than in villages. Of course, this is an overall picture, and facilities will be less readily available to many in the less densely populated areas.

Education: Levels of education at Key Stage 2, 3 and 4 are higher in rural than in urban areas, and 59 per cent of rural schoolchildren achieve five or more GCSEs at grades A* to C, compared with 47 per cent of urban pupils.

Entrepreneurship and business health: A higher proportion of the rural population is self-employed (14.5 per cent compared with 11.8 per cent in urban areas), and this is also reflected in a higher number of businesses (415 per 10,000 population, compared with an urban rate of 379). Perhaps more important, the stock of business continues to grow faster in rural areas (+1.1 per cent contrasted with 0.6 per cent), despite a 3.4 per cent fall in the rural agriculture/fishing sector.

Clearly this is a brief and somewhat selective list, and within the generally positive picture there are negative elements, which will be tackled below. The overall picture, however, is not one of general rural degeneration and deprivation. There are large differences between rural areas, but the greatest economic and social problems seem to be found more in urban areas, notably inner-city ones, where far more people live. For example, in 2003 there were 409 urban wards with an average household income of less than £20,000 compared with only 81 rural wards. The number of households deemed to be in income poverty in urban areas in 2003 was 15.5 million, against 6.0 million in rural areas.

Agriculture and rural areas

So far agriculture has received little attention in this paper. This is because, as an employer and generator of economic activity, in the countryside in general it is a minor player. Nevertheless, it occupies four-fifths of the land area and is thus highly important in terms of landscape and other environmental issues. Statistics on agricultural land use demonstrate that there is no large-scale switch away from farming; between 1996 and 1998 the loss was 11,400 hectares (0.1 per cent), with the largest proportions going into forestry, open land, water, housing, and transport and infrastructure.

Though the problems of the countryside cover a far more extensive range of issues than farming, it is reasonable to include the problems faced by farmers within the review of countryside policy. But the perception of these problems depends very much on who you are within the very diverse agricultural industry.

The causes of the long-run economic pressures on farming – the treadmill of technological advance leading to increases in supply which encounter a relatively static demand – are too well known to need repeating in detail here. On top of the trends are economic shocks that precipitate change or, occasionally, stop it for a period. Recent examples include swift shifts in the relative value of sterling, food safety scares and the 2001 foot-and-mouth disease outbreak (the latter is discussed at length in Chapter 8). The outcome has been has been a cost-price squeeze faced by agricultural producers and declining but unstable incomes. For many decades these have led to inevitable structural changes in the farming industry. Decline in the total number of farms has reflected a net position of rises among the largest agricultural holdings and falls among the smaller ones, with a watershed of zero net change that has been gradually rising over time. An interesting feature is that when farms are put on the market much of the land has been bought by large or medium farms, so that the 'spare' farmhouse and a few hectares of land become a residential unit but appear in the statistics as an increase in the number of very small holdings. Labour has been shed from agriculture, particularly regular hired workers. Though the numbers of farmers are far more stable, a higher proportion is now recorded as part-time. Much of this reflects the pattern of entry into and exit from agriculture, with a higher share of newly established farmers being pluri-active than those they replace.

Pluri-activity – the combining of agriculture with some other gainful activity, mostly off the farm – has always characterised households engaged in farming, and there seems to be no occupation that is not found carried on in parallel with it. Examples of those so engaged range from major industrialists, lawyers, doctors and pop stars at one end of the income spectrum to schoolteachers (often spouses), postmen and manual workers at the other. Though pluri-activity is found mostly among people who occupy small farms, an element of it can be found throughout the size range. The motives behind it are almost as varied as the people who undertake it. The domestic advantages of living on a farm for many are often a major factor. Some will be former full-time farmers who have looked for ways of coping with income fluctuations, but many will have bought there way in after having pursued an outside career. Some may have found themselves in agriculture more or less by accident – such as the farmer's child with an outside profession who inherits the land.

Inheritance illustrates another important characteristic of agriculture in England – the overwhelming majority of farms are run as sole proprietorships or partnerships (unincorporated businesses) in which life-cycle issues are of prominence. Passing your farm to the next generation is an aim of major importance to the present cohort of farmers. Whether it is of much economic importance for society as a whole is far less certain, though it is worth noting that major structural changes often occur at the point at which one management takes over from another, including when younger generations succeed their parents. This affects not only pluri-activity but decisions on farm enlargement, changes of main enterprises and other land-use issues that have environmental implications.

The way in which the operators of farms behave, including their response to policy signals, is not exclusively to do with agriculture. Rather, this will depend on the overall flow of resources towards them and the full array of opportunities open to them. The viability of farms cannot be satisfactorily explained by looking only at what farmers make from farming. Nor can their pattern of investment on and off the farm, land use and spending on improving the environment. Regrettably, statistics on the overall income situation of the agricultural community in England are notoriously sparse. Plenty of information is to hand on the profitability of farming activity, but this gives only part of the picture of what is at the disposal of farm households. It leaves out the profits from other business run on or (more frequently) off the farm, professional earnings, salaried or waged employment, interest, rents, pensions, etc. enjoyed by many farm households, especially (though by no means exclusively) those that operate smaller farms. These income flows frequently transform the level of income of the farm household and reduce instability; indeed, the income generated by the farm may be insignificant or irrelevant; its viability is dependent on what is earned elsewhere. In the USA more than four-fifths of the household income of farm operators comes from non-farm sources, and a relatively small proportion are mainly dependent on farming for their livelihoods. There is little reason why the situation in England should be very different, though much depends on where the boundary of what constitutes a farm operator is drawn. What limited evidence exists (summarised in Hill, 2000) suggests that farm households are, as a group, rather well off in terms of their current incomes, and substantially better off in terms of their wealth than the national average. This is not to say that there are no low-income, low-wealth farm families, but that these are likely to be a relatively small sector of the industry, typically tenant farmers on small farms in parts of the country where alternative employment and income opportunities are scarce.

Policy reform constitutes one type of economic shock to agriculture. In the UK (as in other EU member states subject to the Common Agricultural Policy) agricultural policy has primarily acted as a cushion against the fundamental economic forces at work, defending farmers against the inevitable cost-price squeeze though by no means nullifying it. The main mechanism has been intervention in the market for agricultural products using support buying, export subsidies, import taxes and quantitative restrictions (notably, milk quotas). This system has inevitably led to most of the benefit accruing to the larger producers and owners of land, the factor least elastic in supply. The transfer efficiency to farm households in greatest need has been notoriously low (OECD, 2003). Since 1992 the way in which defensive support has been delivered has been shifted. The MacSharry reforms started this by cutting the support prices of some major commodities (notably cereals and beef), compensating farmers with an array of direct payments (per hectare or per animal). In the event, buoyant market prices meant that the cushioning was unnecessary and these payments resulted in over-compensation. At the same time, though far less generously funded, there has been an attempt to assist agriculture to adjust to the basic realities by providing grants towards restructuring, including for modernising the farm business, training, improvements in marketing, and early retirement schemes for older farmers.

The introduction of a Single Payment Scheme in 2005 (to replace a number of commodity-specific subsidies) – also referred to as the Single Farm Payment – continues the stream of compensation support but is intended to lead to agriculture being more market oriented. Under this system, support will be largely decoupled from production decisions, though it will still be necessary to occupy agricultural land. The effect on farmers and farming systems is hard to predict, though initial research suggests that among some types this will lead to a general reduction in the use of inputs and thus a less intensive use of land, with environmental benefits. In dairying, however, there may be further intensification and thus the danger of negative environmental changes. For the many operators of farms where agriculture is only a minor income source, any shift is likely to be of little economic importance. The uncertain but probably diverse impacts require close monitoring of farm and farm household behaviour in the early stages.

Policies for rural areas

As was noted above, the perceived concerns about the countryside fall into two sets – first, the quality of life of the people who live in the countryside (including farm households) and, second, the quality of the contribution the countryside makes to the environment. These are a mix of market failure and equity issues, with more than a touch of government failure and political economy contributing to them. In England, the socio-economic conditions of rural residents are in general rather satisfactory, as judged by the available indicators, though there are distributional issues that result in deprivation for particular groups of people. Some of the perceived problems are a function of geographical separation, which is an inherent part of much of the countryside and which may be a positive attraction for some people. Environmental problems exist, but most of these seem to be well recognised now and are being brought under control. Nevertheless, it is reasonable to ask whether the policies that we currently have in place address the issues in a satisfactory way. Can adjustments be made that will make policy more effective, efficient or economic? Do we need an interventionist policy at all?

The aims of the government department with primary responsibility for the countryside – Defra – form a convenient starting point for looking at present policies. Though Defra's responsibilities are broader rural issues, it can be argued that almost all of

Box 3 **Defra objectives, 2003–06**

Objective I: Protect and improve the rural, urban, marine and global environment, and lead integration of these with other policies across government and internationally.

Objective II: Enhance opportunity and tackle social exclusion in rural areas.

Objective III: Promote a sustainable, competitive and safe food supply chain which meets consumers' requirements.

Objective IV: Promote sustainable, diverse, modern and adaptable farming through domestic and international actions.

Objective V: Promote sustainable management and prudent use of natural resources domestically and internationally.

Objective VI: Protect the public's interest in relation to environmental impacts and health, and ensure high standards of animal health and welfare.

Source: Spending Review 2002 White Paper

its current six departmental objectives (see Box 3) for the period 2003–06 (arising from the 2002 Spending Review), its ten Public Service Agreements targets (see Annex 2) and the related 31 Service Delivery Agreements negotiated with the Treasury are of relevance to what happens in the countryside.

Resources used by rural policies

A striking feature of the policies currently in place is that they result in a very lopsided balance in terms of the amounts of resources absorbed by, on the one hand, agriculture and, on the other, everything else, though it is difficulty to quantify the situation in a precise way. Some elements are relatively straightforward, such as the amounts of public spending received by individuals and businesses engaged in agriculture and forestry – activities that help define the countryside. These can be augmented by estimates of other transfers made through manipulating markets for agricultural commodities, such as controls on imports and quantitative restrictions (such as milk quotas). The OECD makes regular calculations of the Producer Support Estimate (PSE) to agriculture that covers such elements and reports annually. The value of tax concessions granted to agriculture ('tax expenditures'), however, are substantial but rarely adequately accounted for (OECD, 2004). There is dispute over whether general services to the industry, such as the provision of specialist education in agricultural colleges and free advice to farmers on pollution control, should be included.

But when the recipients are not farmers (occupiers of agricultural land) or landowners or foresters, the situation becomes rather tricky. Many of the socio-economic problems suffered by the people who live in the countryside are the subject of general policies at national or sub-national levels (health, education, policing, etc.). Nevertheless, some of these concessions may give special support to rural areas in the provision of services within a general delivery system (payments to operators of rural bus services, rural medical practices and pharmacies, rural post offices, etc.), which enables some quantification of public spending specifically targeted at rural areas to be made.

Evidence gathered on the budgetary cost (only) of rural policies in the late 1980s, covering all departments of central government with public spending directed at rural land uses or otherwise labelled as rural within administration systems (including spending by national parks authorities), enabled an analysis to be made by policy objective, recipient, sector, etc. (Hill et al., 1989). This found that, among the intended beneficiaries, farmers were clearly the main target group. They absorbed 92 per cent of the £2,301 million of spending encountered. In terms of ultimate objectives, income support to farmers accounted for four-fifths of all spending, but not all of this went directly to them: just over half was received by traders and processors (60 per cent, or 54 per cent of total support). Farmers saw directly only some 27 per cent. Price support (of agricultural products) was the immediate objective of 65 per cent of spending, followed by direct payments to farmers (19 per cent). Altogether, the departments and agencies concerned primarily with agriculture administered 94 per cent of the total support going to rural areas. Interestingly, the analysis showed that it is not correct to assume that financial support to agricultural and forestry activity goes only to recipients living in rural areas: at least some agricultural payments were received by producers at addresses that were distinctly urban in nature. Later figures on a similar basis are hard to come by, though an analysis for 1999/2000 of public expenditure on rural areas in England by broad programme found that agriculture, fisheries and food accounted for 84 per cent of the total (Cabinet Office, 2000). Statistically, things have been eased to some extent by the way in which much of rural policy has been organised since 2000.

The England Rural Development Programme, 2000–06

As part of the agricultural policy reform, the Agenda 2000 package recognised rural development as the 'second pillar' of the Common Agricultural Policy (CAP), the other pillar being the traditional commodity regimes. The Rural Development Regulation 1257/1999 provided for various forms of support, part-funded from the EU budget, which are implemented by Rural Development Programmes (RDPs) for the period 2000–06, drawn up and administered at national level.

In reality, RDPs are to do with far more than rural development seen in the economic sense, being more of a convenient container for various types of policy actions that are not directly associated with commodity production. Thus support for agri-environment schemes and payments to producers in hill areas come under this heading. The amount available to England reflected both the sums available to the UK, determined by factors that included the historic usage of previous forms of structural support, and allocations between the devolved administrations for Wales, Scotland and Northern Ireland. The relatively low utilisation of previous possibilities led to the planned RDP spending per hectare of land for the period 2000–06 in the UK being the lowest in the EU (LUPG, 2002).

The England Rural Development Programme (ERDP) has two priorities: (a) creation of a productive and sustainable rural economy, and (b) conservation and enhancement of the rural environment. It has been implemented by a suite of grant schemes falling into two groups (Project-based Schemes and Land-based Schemes) that are based on the chapters of the RDR 1257/1999 (See Box 4).

Project-based Schemes, set up in 2000, help develop rural businesses and the people involved in them through funding individual projects:

Box 4 Support under Rural Development Regulation 1257/1999

Chapter I – investment in agricultural holdings (covering on-farm investment for reducing production costs, improving and redeploying production, quality improvement, improving the natural environment, hygiene conditions and animal welfare standards, and (on-farm) diversification).

Chapter II – setting up young farmers (i.e. those aged under 40, where the holding is viable and where the person is the head of the holding). Neither England nor Wales has chosen to apply schemes under this chapter, one factor being the smallness of the sums that could be paid in relation to the costs of new entry. Nevertheless, Wales has encouraged young farmers by providing higher rates of support under other schemes.

Chapter III – support for vocational training (of persons engaged in agriculture and forestry – and not limited to landholders). The main method used in England and Wales has been to conduct skills checks and then provide finance to the *providers* of training for setting up training schemes.

Chapter IV – early retirement of elderly farmers (55 years and over but not of normal retirement age) and with assistance for farm transfer, but with support also for an income to farm workers. Neither England nor Wales has chosen to implement schemes, the main arguments against being very high deadweight, low additionality and the very large sums that might be involved. Also there has been a feeling of inequity, in that similar schemes are not available in other occupations.

Chapter V – less favoured areas (LFAs) and areas with environmental restrictions (area payments on land deemed to be of LFA status). In effect, this means a supplementary area payment (Hill Farming Allowance) to farmers in LFAs, with a differentiation between those in Disadvantaged Areas and those in Severely

Disadvantaged Areas. Payments of a similar nature, given for a mix of environmental and social reasons (population maintenance in hill areas), have been given in the United Kingdom since at least 1975.

Chapter VI – agri-environment (the only category in which it is mandatory to offer schemes). The assistance is intended to promote ways of using land which are compatible with the protection and improvement of the environment, the upkeep of the landscape, the use of environmental planning in farming practice, etc. In England this has formed the basis of the Countryside Stewardship Scheme, and payments to farmers in Environmentally Sensitive Areas. An Organic Farming Scheme falls under this chapter.

Chapter VII – improving processing and marketing of agricultural products (grants mostly to non-farmer firms). England applies the Processing and Marketing Grant Scheme, and Wales a similar scheme but subdivided into small grants and others.

Chapter VIII – forestry (including woodland creation by planting and natural regeneration, management of forests and provision of income support for a run of years when land is switched from agricultural use to forestry). England has the Woodland Grant Scheme and the Farm Woodland Premium Scheme (the former to do with operations such as planting and the latter concerned with income compensation).

Chapter IX – promoting the adaptation and development of rural areas (including land reparcelling, setting up farm relief and farm management services, marketing of quality agricultural products, basic services for the rural economy and population, renovation of villages and conservation of the rural heritage, diversification of agricultural activities and those close to agriculture to provide multiple activities or alternative incomes, encouragement for tourism and craft activities, etc.)

- Rural Enterprise Scheme (RES) – in practice largely confined to farmers;
- Processing and Marketing Grant (PMG);
- Vocational Training Scheme (VTS);
- Energy Crops Scheme (ECS) – focused on the production of miscanthus; offers grants for setting up producer groups

Land-based Schemes help conserve and improve the rural environment through funding for land management. These schemes already existed separately before the ERDP, though some were improved or expanded. A modification was introduced in March 2005 when a new scheme (the Environmental Stewardship Scheme) replaced two existing ones.

- Countryside Stewardship Scheme (CSS; replaced from March 2005 by the Environmental Stewardship Scheme);
- Environmentally Sensitive Areas Scheme (ESAS; replaced from March 2005 by the Environmental Stewardship Scheme);
- Organic Farming Scheme (OFS);
- Hill Farm Allowance (HFA);
- Farm Woodland Premium Scheme (FWPS);
- Woodland Grant Scheme (WGS) (works with the Energy Crops Scheme (ECS) and Short Rotation Coppicing (SRC))

Some observations are relevant in the present context. Though made for the English RDP, many are equally applicable to the separate Welsh RDP and its evaluation (Agra CEAS, 2003). First, implementation of the RDP through these schemes is *not* the result of a fundamental re-examination of the problems of rural areas and the design of an appropriate policy response comprising a coherent and synergistic set of actions. Rather, much of the RDP comprised a repackaging of existing policy instruments (with some adjustments) that had originated in piecemeal fashion to meet particular sets of circumstances. The independent evaluation of the England RDP at its mid-term stage concluded that the rationale for some of the schemes needed reconsideration (ADAS/SQW, 2003).

Second, the RDP is very agri-centric, with farmers or landowners accounting for the vast majority of the beneficiaries of the schemes and their financial allocation. This is understandable, given the origins of rural development as a second pillar nested within the Common Agricultural Policy. Even grants for processing and marketing largely focus on agricultural products. Other businessmen in rural areas in theory have the opportunity to bid for funds under the Rural Enterprise Scheme, and groups from the rural community can seek support for village initiatives, rural infrastructure and so on. In reality, however, farmers and landowners have been the main participants in RDP schemes and the group that has seen its income assisted. Even among the schemes that have a primarily environmental focus there is a beneficial effect on incomes in the large majority of cases (ibid.). Income enhancement may not be an aim of the payments to farmers for undertaking environment-enhancing management practices or investments, yet it seems to be an inevitable consequence of offering financial incentives. By targeting such a narrow group of beneficiaries, the broader needs of rural areas are not being addressed by the RDP.

Third, spending on rural development is small in relation to the total cost of supporting agriculture. Under the RDP spending on agri-environment schemes and payments to farmers in hill areas are included, and if these are taken out there is very little that relates to development (as opposed to conservation and protection). According to figures published in *Agriculture in the United Kingdom* (Defra, 2004c: Table 13.1), total public spending on agriculture (UK) was forecast as £3,117 million in the accounting year 2002/03. Of this, £2,622 million (84 per cent) was direct subsidies on agricultural products (mainly arable area payments and livestock subsidies) and other market support, all of it 100 per cent funded by the EU budget. Of the remaining £495 million (16 per cent), most was spent on agri-environment and conservation schemes (£265 million) and on payments to farmers in less favoured (hill and mountain) areas (£188 million), leaving only small amounts for other rural schemes (£10 million) and diversification and capital grants (£10 million). The last two points taken together help explain the comments of the 2003 evaluators that, even in terms of its own objectives, the programme was generally more effective in addressing its environmental aim than that of creating a productive and sustainable rural economy (ADAS/ SQW, 2003). The introduction of the Single Farm Payment in 2005, though changing the form in which support is given to agriculture by very largely removing the link with the present level of farm production (being, in effect, compensation based on historic receipts), does not alter the dominance by agriculture of public money directed at the countryside.

Other policies affecting the countryside

But policy that impinges on rural areas is not exclusively that of either the first or second (rural development) pillars of agricultural policy. In Wales EU Regional Policy is important. Areas designated as Objective 1 regions (those lagging behind and given special economic support) account for about half the national area and include many counties (unitary authorities) that are regarded as rural, but that complication is far less significant in England and will not be considered further here.

Some other general policies, however, are important to rural areas in England. The breadth of the economic base in rural areas means that what happens in non-agricultural industries can be of far more importance to incomes and employment for the people living there than the health of the farming industry, though the secondary linkages should not be underestimated (the impact of controls during the 2001 foot-and-mouth disease outbreak on tourism is a case in point). Macroeconomic conditions (inflation, interest rates, exchange rates, etc.) will affect rural as well as urban businesses. Many social policies that apply horizontally without differentiation between rural and urban areas, such as old-age pension levels and family credits, will be significant for the quality of life in the countryside, and some disproportionately so because of the demographic profile of the rural population.

As mentioned above, some general policies incorporate special provisions for delivery in rural areas, where remoteness and population sparsity present problems. Even when these do not feature, it is important for their implications for rural areas to be considered if harmful effects are to be avoided. The government has introduced 'rural proofing' to increase the attention given to the rural dimension in such policies (Countryside Agency, 2004c). The aim is to encourage policy-makers to systematically think about whether there will be any significant differential impacts in rural areas; and if there are, to assess what these might be, and to consider what adjustments or compensations might be made to fit rural circumstances. The Countryside Agency annually requests information from twelve departments of central government and eight regional Government Offices (not including the Government Office for London). The third annual report (for 2003/04) found that some departments had good evidence that rural proofing was taking place, but with some weak performers. Evidence of tangible outcomes of the process was rather patchy and elusive. One contributing factor was the lack of a rural marker in many departmental data-sets, something that the new definition of rural, discussed above, is intended to help remedy.

Most of the above policies involve budgetary expenditure. But there are others that do not which nevertheless are significant to both the socio-economic and environmental aspects of the countryside. A few examples must suffice. Taxation is one. The exclusion of agricultural land and property from business taxes, together with other provisions for operating a business, means that there are substantial attractions for people with other sources of income in living on and operating a farm (not necessarily on a commercial basis) and passing wealth between generations in this form. Planning controls are another – these have proved to be a brake on the ability of farmers to diversify their businesses, though there have been suggestions that the special provisions for permitting the construction of farm service accommodation may have been operated to their advantage. The taxation of second homes, while not exclusively a rural issue, none the less carries special resonance for villages, where it is often felt that they have contributed to putting house prices beyond the means of local inhabitants (see the chapters by Stockdale and Meadowcroft later in this collection). Other examples are legislation on official designations of environmental features that carry with them restriction on land use (for example, EU Directives on conservation areas and wild bird habitats that give rise to Natura 2000 sites or national designations, such as Sites of Special Scientific Interest), on water quality and on access. Some of these can be highly politically sensitive.

To sum up this section, it appears that the countryside is subject to a wide range of policy interventions, some general, which have special implications for rural areas, some variants of general policies, and some specifically aimed at the resources found in rural areas and the activities carried on there. Though it is difficult to be precise, it appears that, of the financial resources devoted to policies that are de facto rural, a very large proportion goes on supporting agricultural producers, followed by payment to land users and owners under the guise of them providing environmental services. The wisdom of this distribution of resources is, at least, open to question.

Sustainability and policy

A great deal is made in the rhetoric of UK rural and agricultural strategy documents of 'sustainability'. In 2002, Defra's policy document *The Strategy for Sustainable Farming and Food* (Defra, 2002a) built on the output of the Policy Commission chaired by Sir Donald Curry, in which the '... vision was of a sustainable, competitive and diverse farming and food sector, playing a dynamic role in the rural economy and delivering effectively and efficiently the environmental goals we as a society set for ourselves'. Sustainability is a concept inherent to agriculture. Indeed, the UK agricultural economist Edgar Thomas commented in a textbook of the 1940s that any process of food production that was not capable of being carried on indefinitely should properly be classified not with agriculture but with mining. In modern usage the term 'agricultural sustainability' has a number of related meanings, and achieving them involves associated challenges; sustainability can be viewed from a number of perspectives – environmental, economic, social, administrative, political, etc.

In *The Strategy for Sustainable Food and Farming*, Defra mentions the three aspects of sustainability that it sees as presenting challenges – economic (with attention given to the incomes squeeze felt by farmers and the low investment in people in the food and drinks industry); environmental (where agriculture creates both positive and negative externalities, and with food packaging waste singled out for mention); and social (while the problems of farmers are mentioned, such challenges are clearly mostly felt in other sectors).[4] When Defra comes to listing the key principles for sustainable food and farming (see Box 5) within this strategy, no mention is given to the support of farm incomes, and the profitability of farming is implied only in two areas – supporting the viability and diversity of rural and urban economies and communities, and enabling viable livelihoods to be made from sustainable land management, for which payments

4   Given that agricultural policy is dominated by the application of the CAP it is instructive to examine the EU's view of sustainability. According to the website of the European Commission: 'Sustainable agriculture in Europe is our means of ensuring that future generations can enjoy the benefits of Europe's unique environmental heritage and natural resources, as we do today. Achieving sustainability, however, means meeting three challenges – an economic challenge (by strengthening the viability and competitiveness of the agricultural sector); a social challenge (by improving living conditions and economic opportunities in rural areas); and an ecological challenge (by promoting good environmental practices as well as the provision of services linked to the maintenance of habitats, biodiversity and landscape).'

Box 5 **Defra's key principles for sustainable farming now and in the future**

- Produce **safe, healthy products** in response to market demands, and ensure that all consumers have access to nutritious food, and to accurate information about food products.
- Support the **viability and diversity of rural and urban** economies and communities.
- Enable viable livelihoods to be made from **sustainable land management**, both through the market and through payments for public benefits.
- Respect and operate within the **biological limits of natural resources** (especially soil, water and biodiversity).
- Achieve consistently high standards of **environmental performance** by **reducing energy consumption**, by minimising resource inputs, and use **renewable energy** wherever possible.
- Ensure a safe and hygienic working environment and high social welfare and training for all employees involved in the food chain.
- Achieve consistently high standards of **animal health and welfare**.
- Sustain the resources available for growing food and supplying other public benefits over time, except where alternative land uses are essential to meet other needs of society.

Note: Bold type in original
Source: Defra (2002a)

are made for providing public (environmental) benefits. Thus, even when the focus is the food chain rather than the broader countryside, it is hard to see how the large share of resources used to provide farm income support corresponds with the declared weight of the various objectives.

Structural sustainability

Because 'sustainability' is so important, it is worth considering aspects of it in more detail. Even for economic sustainability – the prime focus here – there are sub-sets of meanings. First there is the ability of the agricultural industry as presently structured to continue within the economic, technical and policy environment. This might be termed *structural static sustainability*, and reflects the ability of today's farm firms to compete. Any given structure, however, is compatible only with a static environment. In the real world, where markets signal the impact of technological advance and of historical events, such as the reform of agricultural policies, the notion of sustainability has to include the ability of structures to adapt to remain competitive – something that might be termed *structural dynamic sustainability*. The government's aim of developing a competitive and adaptable farming system by implication embraces this dynamic aspect of sustainability.

A key question that policy-makers for the countryside must face is whether their interventions enhance or constrain the ability of the agricultural industry (and the rest of the rural sector) to adjust to changing economic and technical conditions. Of course, both aspects of sustainability may show wide geographical variation, and a marked distinction may arise between regions with small-scale agricultural structures dominated by family farms and those areas where there is a legacy of large-scale agricultural units. And, as noted above, the performance and behaviour of individual farms cannot be explained satisfactorily without taking into account all their economic activities, which, in many cases, extend beyond agriculture. Their ability to survive as independent units is often less dependent on the profitability of farming than on what is happening in the rest of the economy. The sustainability of agriculture cannot be considered in isolation.

Sustainability and multi-functionality

Of particular significance in the sustainability debate is that English farming is recognised as not only producing agricultural commodities but also as the generator of environmental, social and cultural services important to the welfare of society (the so-called *multi-functionality* of the *European model* of agriculture). There is a strand of opinion that believes that the present structure of the industry, dominated by family farms, is better placed than an industry dominated by other types of farm business to provide beneficial environmental and social externalities and public goods associated with agriculture. The family farm is a notoriously imprecise concept (Hill, 1993), and often confuses size of business, size of landholding, family labour input and pattern of business control and ownership, including inter-generational continuity. In reality, it would be difficult to find many English farms, even large ones, that could not be classed as family farms according to ownership criteria. This does not stop the notion of the family farm having substantial political valency, especially when its continued existence is thought to be under threat.

There seems, however, to be a lack of convincing evidence of the strength of any relationship between the existing structure and the desired externalities which might be used to justify protecting the family farm. For example, a relationship may be hypothesised between, on the one hand, family farming and, on the other, environmental benefits. But is the critical factor the farming system employed (the most likely explanation), the size of the farm in terms of area (which may in part determine the farming system) or whether it is family operated?

Turning to arguments that focus on farming's contribution to rural society through generating jobs, income, social interaction and cohesion, is the crucial factor the size of the farm, the number of people working in the farm business, their relationships by blood and marriage, or the household size and incomes of people living in the farm dwelling? If it is the number of people in gainful employment and living on the farm, does it matter whether they are engaged in farming or in diversified activities on the farm, or gaining their income from off-farm activities?

A case might be made that policies to support the present family farm structure are required on social grounds, and monetary values might be attached to the benefits so that they can be compared with the costs of such a policy. But it is by no means certain that the same agricultural structure that provides social externalities to an optimum level is needed to generate environmental benefits to the economic optimum. It may be that land management could be more efficiently operated with far fewer and thus larger farm businesses which could, at the same time, generate satisfactory incomes for their operators.

Sustainability assumes particular importance for agriculture in the upland areas of England, where farming receives not only the payments generally available but also special assistance under the Rural Development Programme for Less Favoured Areas (LFAs – differentiated according to the degree of economic handicap deemed to result from the physical conditions found there). Here economic, social and environmental sustainability are at their most inter-mixed. A recent study (IEEP et al., 2004) has found that many of the social problems faced by people living in LFAs are general in nature – lack of affordable housing for young people and poor public services such as transport, healthcare and education – though some were specific to the farming community, such as illness associated with the rigours of harsh working conditions. The research draws attention to the declining role of agricultural employment and output in LFAs and concludes that the justification for public support for hill farming in agricultural terms appears weak: 'the level of public expenditure required to maintain a relatively small number of jobs and produce primary products appears disproportionately large to the benefits accrued' (ibid.).

The continuation of tourism in many of these areas is, however, fundamental to their future, though the link between the present nature of hill farming and tourism is not well understood. One must conclude that, as with many other activities in these areas, such as grouse shooting, horse riding and food processing and retailing, tourism may be little dependent on hill farming, at least in its present farm structure. Similarly, the positive contribution that hill farmers have made to the communities in which they live appears to have declined, and there are divergent views as to whether they or newcomers make the greater contribution to social sustainability. In contrast, the role of agriculture in helping shape landscape and the diversity of habitats and wildlife is widely recognised, though even here there are both positive and negative aspects to the impacts that hill farming can have and a general lack of analysis of whether it is the farming system or the present structure of hill farming businesses which is the basis of the causal link.

Policy sustainability

Second, running parallel to the various strands of sustainability touched on above, is the concept of *policy sustainability*, which can be described as the ability of the existing array of policy interventions to continue. Even within this context there are shades of meaning. One usage is where the policy initiates a response that continues after the instrument is withdrawn, such as may happen when an investment grant stimulates farm productivity in a way that raises income and leads to higher levels of saving and investment without the need for further assistance. Another usage, more relevant in the present context, is where the cost of the instrument changes in relation to the resources available, an unsustainable policy being one where the costs escalate to the extent that they present budgetary difficulty or are no longer considered commensurate with the benefits created or are in other ways no longer acceptable (such as being raised to political prominence). For example, it may be that the support provided to agriculture as the Single Farm Payment may prove unsustainable, not so much because of the budgetary cost but because with the passage of time it may become politically vulnerable. Given its roots in the 'compensatory payments' of the 1992 CAP reforms, people are increasingly likely to ask why this form of compensation is still necessary, a criticism that can only be sharpened by the release by

Defra of information on the sums paid to individual beneficiaries (under the previous system of direct payments). When large sums are received by prominent individuals and firms not in obvious need of support, questions are bound to arise as to the rationale for such public expenditure.

The shape of a more efficient and less inhibiting policy for rural areas

To summarise the main points so far:

- The problems associated with the countryside arise from a mix of causes that relate market failure, equity issues and government failure.
- All three can be manifested in economic, environmental and social ways.
- The economic and social problems of the countryside, though rarely unique, are increasingly well documented, with institutions set up and dedicated to monitoring them.
- Rural areas differ greatly in the type and severity of the social and economic problems faced.
- Different groups living in rural areas will see problems differently, with social exclusion strongly linked to low incomes.
- Land use in rural areas is a major factor in determining environmental quality for society in general (not only for those who live in rural areas).
- Agriculture and forestry, as the main land users in the countryside, have a major role to play in achieving environmental goals, which will also vary greatly between

areas. This role is particularly sensitive in the hills and uplands.

- Agriculture can play only a small direct role as an agent in assisting with economic and social problems.
- At present the large majority of public resources directed at the countryside appear to benefit agricultural producers and landowners, and this is likely to be an imbalance. Historic factors are the main explanation for this, especially the UK's membership of the EU and of its CAP and the fact that EU rural policy has one of its main roots within agricultural policy.
- Even within support to the agricultural industry, the greater part of spending relates to the past production of agricultural commodities rather than to present agricultural or rural policy objectives.

At the outset of this paper questions were posed, somewhat rhetorically, about the need for a policy and the shape it might take. A highly detailed specification of problems and responses is not feasible here. Rather, in the light of the above points, what can be done is to set out what might be looked for in a policy for the countryside that would be an improvement in terms of effectiveness, efficiency and economy, the traditional 'three Es' of the evaluator. A number of characteristics present themselves.

A more rational policy

There is room for re-examining the rationale for having a policy for the countryside that attempts to intervene and change outcomes. Are there market failures that, in principle, might justify intervention on *economic* grounds? If so, this does not necessarily mean that there is something to be gained from using public resources to correct for this failure. The most efficient policy might be to do nothing. Or is the basic rationale one of *equity* – such as fair access to services – or some form of *political economy* thinking, for example where a policy needs to be pursued in order to achieve more significant reforms elsewhere. The sections that follow look at policy from each of these perspectives.

Production of market goods

In terms of *commodity production*, the rhetoric for achieving a sustainable agriculture focuses on the competitiveness of farms, an argument that can be extended to other sectors. If firms in rural areas are not competitive, is it because there are information gaps, sticky prices, factor immobility or other problems that, once corrected, will enable them to become competitive not just in the present economic conditions but also able to adjust to future signals? What are the costs to society resulting from this form of market imperfection in terms of the GDP forgone?

In the case of English agriculture it seems that farm land made available by people exiting the industry is absorbed by other farmers (mainly medium and larger operators, because they can spread fixed costs, keeping land prices high). Following structural adjustment, aggregate supply would be more likely to rise than fall. Of course, any such additional output would need to be valued not at prices distorted upwards by CAP support but at levels (usually lower) that reflect what could be achieved on world markets. But even if there were an economic cost to society from such sources of market failure, the decision to intervene on efficiency grounds would have to be on the basis of a comparison with the value to society of resources used elsewhere. If no effective mechanism can be found to overcome the forces currently restricting output (early retirement schemes for elderly farmers have never proved very successful in England), or the costs exceed the benefits, the efficient policy option is to do nothing.

This efficiency argument is independent of the private costs borne by the individual farm when it has to adjust. No doubt, if farmers or other operators in rural areas are forced to adjust by shedding resources, even to close down, they and their staff face problems of loss of income and asset values, of finding alternative employment for their resources, even changing location and moving home, but these do not necessarily mean that there will be a cost to society in terms of lost GDP.

Thus there may still be *equity* reasons to justify intervention with the production of market goods. When dealing with issues of competitiveness, it is usually judged reasonable for some cushioning to be offered if government policy suddenly changes tack. For example, if farm operators have been accustomed to receiving support for their production of agricultural commodities, and have planned their investments in the reasonable expectation that this support would continue, fairness might suggest some compensation so that their private costs are shared with the rest of society. Whether this be for income denied or for capital losses, or as a stream or lump sum, will depend on circumstances. But it would not be reasonable for this compensation to be expected ad infinitum. It would be time-limited and paid to the people who suffered from the change unconditionally (the present Single Farm Payment operated in England from 2005 fails on both counts, being open ended and requiring a link with agricultural land).

Equity also underlies the rationale for policies countering

economic exclusion, such as lack of access to services resulting from geographic separation, deemed to be felt in particular by low-income rural groups. The centre of the problem is income distribution. The prospect of paying higher pensions and social benefits to people in the countryside has some logic but is unlikely to find favour as it calls attention to the lack of equity between the treatment of low-income cases in town and those in the country-side. Subsidising the providers of services (rural public transport, pharmacies, clinics, shops, etc.) has attractions as a policy delivery system, particularly where it is known that the users are predom-inantly the target group (affluent incomers are less likely to use rural buses). But such support has to be looked at alongside the alternative of creating ways in which relatively poor rural dwellers can earn more.

A third line of rationale for policy is *political economy*. When applied to the narrow topic of reforming agricultural policy, it is clear that the introduction of forms of direct payment to farmers in 1992 was in large part a necessary cost of securing the reforms proposed by Commissioner MacSharry, a first step that opened up the prospect of far more fundamental changes. They were also in part compensation for an anticipated loss of income from the market as support prices were cut substantially. In this context, the obfuscation by EU policy-makers on the possible duration of such payments can be seen as a ploy to maximise political support for them.

Non-market services

Where market failures take the form of economic externalities and lack of public goods, the policy approach needed is to internalise them, in the sense that they are taken into account in farmers' resource allocation decisions in a way that results in social-welfare maximising levels of non-commodity outputs. The *efficiency* argument is less easy to pursue because of the difficulty of valuing non-market goods and services. It is not satisfactory to assume that marginal changes in biodiversity and landscape are beyond price. Policy decisions clearly rank them less than this, though the political system in England has raised their implicit value in recent decades.

When looking for a better policy for the countryside, rather than pursuing the issue of valuing environmental services, it would seem more productive (at least in the short term) to focus on the search for interventions that achieved the desired aims at least resource cost – the pursuit of economy (rather than efficiency). For example, in hill areas maintaining the existing number of farmers by supporting their incomes may be wasteful of resources if the real relationship with landscape character is the farming system, which might be preserved at far lower cost by fewer but larger farms. Similarly, though ways of valuing the quality of community vibrancy are open to dispute (and, judged by demographics, there seems to be no shortage of people willing to move to the country-side), there is plenty of opportunity to challenge the way in which this is promoted. The rationale of supporting hill farming as a way of sustaining rural communities might be far weaker than that of supporting a village pub or post office.

Also, within this examination of economy it is important to reflect on the delivery system, such as the gains that might result from instruments that involved producers bidding to supply the socially determined desired level of environmental services, in contrast to an approach designed to compensate them for the estimated marginal costs of providing them. It is worth noting that the bidding system, which reflects the opportunity costs of individual land users, appears to be within the 'Green Box' of the latest Doha round of World Trade Organisation discussions, whereas the cost-offsetting option does not (Blandford and Hill, 2004). At present few schemes under England's RDP involve bidding.

Equity figures as part of the rationale for policy covering some non-market goods, such as access to the countryside for recreation. At a larger level, the special assistance given by the EU's Structural Funds to regions lagging behind (many of which are rural) is in part driven by the feeling that the people there have the right to share in the increasing well-being of the rest, though it is difficult to separate out the income/consumption element from the cultural and social. For non-market goods *political economy* issues can be part of the underlying rationale of some elements of policy for the countryside. A classic case is the public funding of non-governmental organisations (NGOs) primarily active in environmental protection, to provide a counter-weight to the well-funded interest groups of businesses that may be perceived to cause harm (for example, under the EU's Community Action Programme (Decision 466/2002)).

Objectives of higher quality

Policy for the countryside, and especially for agriculture, has suffered from a general lack of clarity and testability, with a failure to separate multiple objectives. In line with probing the rationale, the objectives of rural policy must be expressed in a way that relates better to the aims of policy. Given that income support of farmers is the main purpose of the spending channelled to rural areas under the CAP, it might be expected that targets would exist, such as minimum household incomes for farm operators, or the percentage of farm households falling below some poverty line. In reality, not only is there no clear statement of the income objectives of agricultural policy, there is not even any reliable evidence on the household income of English farmers. Such information could lead to more specific objectives and a more efficient policy. But, assessing incomes in ways that are in general use for exposing poverty raises the question of whether a sector-specific policy is justified; *why should low-income farmers be treated differently from other poor people?* If, as seems likely judging by international experience (Hill, 2000; OECD, 2003), the operators of English farms as a group turn out to have household incomes that compare favourably with the rest of society (though much comes from sources other than farming) – and they also emerge as rather wealthier – then the drive for better objectives will inevitably raise serious questions about the need for the income support that underlies present agricultural policy.

Attention to quality should also result in a more careful distinction being made between intermediate and final objectives and to testing the links between them. Taking the support of hill farming as an example, the aims of the special payments (Hill Farming Allowances) in the Rural Development Programme (embedded in Rural Development Regulation 1257/1999) are to do with conserving the environment and keeping people living there, though the intermediate objective is to compensate operators for the handicaps they suffer by attempting to farm in these areas. There is no guarantee that making payments based on area (formerly on numbers of animals) achieves either environmental or social objectives in an economic way.

Where interventions have multiple objectives, separating them and examining how each might be achieved more efficiently may save resources. A critical review of the objectives for support to hill farming might conclude that, in some cases, environmental improvement might come from leaving the land unfarmed, or reducing the numbers of businesses trying to extract a livelihood from it and the intensity with which the land is used ('ranching'). The social aims might be served more economically by other instruments; for example, the retention of relatively low-income young local people in upland villages might be achieved more effectively and at lower resource cost through planning control mechanisms, which could influence the supply of suitable accommodation and facilitate the conversion of redundant agricultural buildings to provide premises for non-agricultural businesses.

Resource allocation and balance

At present the greater part of spending on rural support goes to agriculture. On the surface there seems little connection between the present balance and the aims of the government's *Rural Strategy 2004* of 'Economic and social regeneration', 'Social justice for all' and 'Enhancing the value of our countryside'. Even when looking at the government policy aims for the farming and food sector alone, there must be unease at the present allocation, with some 84 per cent of Defra support to agriculture in 2002/03 going on direct payments and market support. Most of these payments to farm operators are compensations under the CAP for policy changes, some of which took place a considerable time ago. Rather than encouraging agriculture to become more competitive and thus more sustainable, these payments cushion farmers against fundamental economic forces and endanger the longer-term economic sustainability of the industry.

While the present allocation can be explained by historic factors, it is very probably sub-optimal in terms of social welfare. It is difficult to be categorical about this. Imbalance is a matter of resources in relation to need at the margin, which is difficult to establish, especially when the impacts can stretch long into the future. Nevertheless, an improvement in the efficiency of resource use would be expected to come from a freer and better-informed choice between the different ways of allocating public funds, of which agriculture would be only one. If the rationale for some of the agricultural payments can be demonstrated to be weak, then not only does reallocation look attractive, but also the overall sums spent may be lowered.

Some rebalancing of spending on agriculture by switching funds received from the EU towards 'rural development' schemes is possible already – the UK is allowed to use 'modulation' to divert a proportion of direct payments to increase resources for environmental spending (and to supplement them with national funds). A freer choice could be beneficial. The use of funds to assist farmers to adapt to economic and technical conditions must, however, be treated with caution. International experience suggests that the ability of farm operators to adjust to even quite large economic shocks is commonly underestimated (Blandford and Hill, 2004). Two key factors in facilitating this process are an effective market in land (ownership and/or rental) and the quality of human capital of farm families, not just their transferable skills but also their level of general education. Both can be heavily affected by factors outside the normal realm of agricultural decision-makers – such as capital taxation and educational policy. Many of the more major changes, such as farm enlargement or the decision to combine an off-farm job with agriculture, are particularly associated with inter-generational transfers of the business (the main route for exit from and entry to farming). Schemes aimed at improving the performance of individual farm businesses and enhancing skills may represent an efficient use of resources at the margin, though it must be conceded that early retirement schemes for English farmers have not performed well.

It has to be recognised that most of the changes that have taken place in the structure of agriculture have *not* been assisted by public funds. Perhaps the more important purpose for such schemes is their political economy role; by concentrating attention on them and providing modest amounts of additional resources, more radical reform in the commodity support and direct payment systems becomes politically acceptable.

Diversity

Early in this paper a question was raised about whether a distinct policy for the countryside is justified – whether the diversity of rural and urban environments required a differentiated approach. For aspects of policy concerned with the state of natural resources in rural areas, the need for a separate set of policies is almost self-evident. It is hard to conceive of a policy on land use that could easily address both rural and urban concerns effectively. On economic and social matters, however, the case is far less obvious. Agriculture as a gainful activity has lost much of its uniqueness. Many farm operators are already well diversified and thus share both the advantages and disadvantages of operating in the countryside faced by other firms based there. And while there are concerns with living conditions in rural areas, at least for some sectors of the population (access to services, housing, etc.), these are often shared by people living in urban areas, sometimes more acutely. Whether a separate policy for these problems in the countryside is justified is almost entirely a matter of pragmatism in the way sets of problems found in different geographical areas are handled by administrations and delivery systems are organised.

Diversity is also found between rural areas, suggesting that, while a national policy framework may be required, a blanket one-size-fits-all approach is inappropriate. Given that economic, environmental and social problems vary widely, in a well-designed policy interventions should also vary in nature and extent from one area to another. When agricultural policy was mainly concerned with commodity markets, it was reasonable to have support regimes that operated not only for the UK as a whole but also for the entire EU market (though in practice for much of the life of the CAP agri-monetary mechanisms prevented a true single market from operating). There is, however, a general move towards more geographical differentiation in agricultural policy. The rural development 'second pillar' of the CAP is operated by four separate programmes in the UK. Under this, additional support for farming is given in less favoured areas, with payments varying according to the degree of disadvantage. Thus, even for agriculture, there is an increasing tendency for policy mechanisms to differentiate between rural areas.

The development of policy that identifies the locally most pressing problems and reacts accordingly implies that some decision-making has to take place at the local level, in line with the general principle of subsidiarity. Encouraging local participation has been a recurring theme in rural development. Flexibility in operation at a local level should not, however, be confused with local administration and financial responsibility. It is not impossible for a centrally administered scheme to incorporate the flexibility needed to tailor for diverse local circumstances – agri-environment schemes show this in operation with a menu-based approach. On the other hand, practicalities may make for a more effective and efficient policy if delivery is organised at a regional or district level. The 'Leader' programme and Rural Community Councils have demonstrated the value of small-scale, bottom-up development initiatives and of harnessing community resources. It seems unlikely that all aspects of policies for the countryside can or should be fragmented to the very local level. Nevertheless, in indicating ways of improving policies for rural areas, it must be concluded that territorially determined sets of responses are needed, in which there is the opportunity to shape actions to needs at the local level.

Can we get to a better policy?

Exposing weaknesses in the rationale and objectives of policies for rural areas is likely to ruffle feathers. Asking questions about the purpose of giving so much public support to agriculture as direct payments in return for uncertain benefits is likely to lead to the conclusion that at least some of what is currently provided should be withdrawn. If the aim is really a competitive and sustainable agriculture, then the market should be allowed to operate in such a way that there is pressure on the uncompetitive and unsustainable units to exit. Such questions are more politically acceptable today than a decade ago, but the protests from interested parties – farmers, landowners and the pressure groups representing them –

still carry weight. Formerly, the Ministry of Agriculture, Fisheries and Food and university departments of agricultural economics might be counted among the vested interests, but these voices have been retoned by restructuring or muted by sectoral shifts. In their place new sensitivities have emerged. Now, questioning the value of the environmental services and social contributions made by agriculture is almost heresy. Probing the assumption that the support given to hill farming in its present form achieves environmental and social goals in an efficient way runs into hot water both from agriculturalists and environmentalists. But an unquestioning approach is as dangerous when related to the multi-functionality of agriculture as it was in the post-war decades, when food security and supposed income problems among farmers were the orthodox explanations for why large transfers were repeatedly made to the farming community.

Reallocation will be eased substantially if the Single Farm Payment (SFP), operational from 2005, comes under increasing criticism as being compensation that is no longer justified and which prevents English agriculture becoming more competitive. As a far more transparent form of support than the old production-based systems, and for which the benefits to society are uncertain, it is politically vulnerable. Defra's decision to publish in early 2005 details of who receives what in direct payments served to draw further attention to the apparent inequities of agricultural support (though, strictly, these figures related to payments that preceded the SFP). If the final link between payments and land is broken (and it seems possible that agreement on this may be achieved in the WTO), then pressure to radically revise the SFP may be too great to ignore. Though complete abandonment is unlikely, transubstantiation into payments for the supply of environmental and social services is highly probable. Already the ground seems to be under preparation by Defra in the form of the 2005 Environmental Stewardship scheme, with its various tiers of payment, the entry level of which appears to correspond with what many farmers are already doing.

Beyond agriculture, questioning the uniqueness of housing problems in the countryside, or rural poverty, or poor access to basic services (where severe problems can also confront people living in city centres), is likely to raise opposition now from the many institutional and professional interests that have been built up in the industry of countryside watchers, monitors and researchers in government agencies, independent charities and academic departments. The issue is not that problems do not exist, but that bureaucracy and pressure groups have institutional and personal interests in keeping the questioning of fundamentals off the agenda of public debate.

Shifting the balance and method of support to policies for the countryside poses practical problems. Most spending under agricultural and rural development policies in England takes place under EU-level legislation; the ability to reallocate funds is severely restricted by present funding rules. Indeed, it may not be in the national interest to seek a more rational and efficient policy as this may result in a negative shift in the balance of contributions and drawing from the EU budget. Administrative capacity is also an issue; while the infrastructure already exists to monitor the economic health of farm businesses and to transfer large sums to them, it is by no means certain that the mechanisms are in place to channel substantially greater volumes of resources to other economic agents that rebalancing might bring.

If some rebalancing takes place, it is likely that regional and local government will need to develop additional roles and capacities to deliver policies, which implies resource costs. This does not mean, however, that all rural policy should be devolved to this local level. Because many of the economic and social problems found in the countryside are not uniquely rural, there is a case for leaving the responsibility for carrying them out in the hands of those government departments for which they are the mainstream activity (health, education, transport, etc.). Horizontal links between departments have always been relatively weak. Defra's pursuit of 'rural proofing' goes some way to managing this situation.

Despite the practical problems, the case for a less sectoral and better-integrated view of economic activity and resource use in the countryside, in which the changed composition of what currently goes on is more fully recognised, is clear. In particular, the role of agriculture should be seen within the larger context of a countryside that is diverse in the ways in which residents earn their livelihoods. But the essential key to a better policy for the countryside is a more critical examination of the real problems found there and a rigorous scrutiny of the performance of the present arrangements used by government. For some problems it may be better to do nothing, letting market mechanisms work their way through. For others, policies radically different from those currently in place offer attractions. By pursuing this approach it should be possible to improve the present inefficient use of public funds.

References

ADAS/SQW (2003), *The Mid-term Evaluation of the England Rural Development Programme*, ADAS Consulting Ltd and SQW Ltd, available on the Defra website.

Agra CEAS (2003), *Mid-term Evaluation of the Rural Development Plan for Wales*, Cardiff: Agra CEAS Consultants Ltd for the Welsh European Funding Office, Agriculture and Rural Affairs Department, National Assembly for Wales.

Blandford, D. and B. Hill (2004), *Facilitating Farm-level Adjustment to the Reform of Domestic Agricultural and Trade Policies*, International Agricultural Trade Research Consortium, Trade Issues paper (in press).

Cabinet Office (1999), *Rural Economies*, London: Cabinet Office.

Cabinet Office (2000), *Sharing the Nation's Prosperity – Economic, social and environmental conditions in the countryside – a report to the Prime Minister*, London: Performance and Innovation Unit, Cabinet Office.

Countryside Agency (2001), *The State of the Countryside 2001*, Cheltenham: Countryside Agency.

Countryside Agency (2004a), *The State of the Countryside 2004*, Cheltenham: Countryside Agency.

Countryside Agency (2004b), *Review of Countryside Issues in England*, Cheltenham: Countryside Agency.

Countryside Agency (2004c), *Rural Proofing in 2003/2004. A report to government by the Countryside Agency*, Cheltenham: Countryside Agency, www.countryside.gov.uk.

Defra (2002a), *The Strategy for Sustainable Farming and Food: Facing the future*, London: Department for Environment, Food and Rural Affairs.

Defra (2002b), *Farming and Food's Contribution to Sustainable Development: Economic and statistical analysis*, London: Department for Environment, Food and Rural Affairs.

Defra (2004a), *Rural Strategy 2004*, London: Department for Environment, Food and Rural Affairs.

Defra (2004b), *Social and Economic Change and Diversity in Rural England*, London: Department for Environment, Food and Rural Affairs.

Defra (2004c), *Agriculture in the United Kingdom*, London: Department for Environment, Food and Rural Affairs.

DETR/MAFF (2000), *Our Countryside: the Future – A fair deal for rural England*, Cm. 4909, London: HMSO for the Department for the Environment, Transport and the Regions.

European Commission (2004), *Proposal for a Council Regulation on Support to Rural Development by the European Agricultural Fund for Rural Development*, COM(2004)490 final.

Haskins, C. (2003), *Rural Delivery Review – A report on the delivery of government policies in rural England*, London: Defra.

Hill, B. (1993), 'The "myth" of the family farm: defining the family farm and assessing its importance in the European Community', *Journal of Rural Studies*, 9(4): 359–70.

Hill, B. (2000), *Farm Incomes, Wealth and Agricultural Policy*, 3rd edn, Aldershot: Ashgate.

Hill, B. (2002), *Determining DEFRA's Rural Statistics – Discussion document*, London: Defra (published on the Defra website).

Hill, B., N. Young and G. Brookes (1989), *Alternative Support Systems for Rural Areas. Report of a research project for the DoE and MAFF*, 2 vols, Ashford: Wye College, Department of Agricultural Economics.

Hodge, I. and M. Whitby (1986), 'The UK: rural development, issues and analysis', *European Review of Agricultural Economics*, 13: 391–413.

IEEP (Institute for European Environmental Policy), Land Use Consultants and GHK Consulting (2004), *An Assessment of the Impacts of Hill Farming in England on Economic, Environmental and Social Sustainability*.

LUPG (2002), *Europe's Rural Futures – The nature of rural development II*, Land Use Policy Group, WWF.

NAC Rural Trust (1987), *Village Homes for Village People*, London: NAC Rural Trust.

OECD (annual), *Agricultural Policies in OECD Countries: Monitoring and evaluation*, Paris: Organisation for Economic Co-operation and Development.

OECD (2003), *Farm Household Income – Issues and policy responses*, Paris: Organisation for Economic Co-operation and Development.

OECD (2004), *Non-sectoral Policies for the Agriculture and Agro-food Sectors: Taxation and social security*, Paris: Organisation for Economic Co-operation and Development.

Roberts, S. (2002) *Key Drivers of Economic Development and Inclusion in Rural Areas, Initial scoping study of the socio-economic evidence base for Defra*, London: Defra.

SERRL et al. (2001a), *A Review of Urban and Rural Area Definitions – Preliminary draft final report*, London: Department of the Environment, Transport and the Regions.

SERRL et al. (2001b), *Review of Urban and Rural Area Definitions – User guide*, London: Department for Transport, Local Government and the Regions.

Annex 1: The government's rural policy objectives (from the Rural White Paper (DETR/MAFF, 2000))

Objective 1

To facilitate the development of dynamic, competitive and sustainable economies in the countryside, tackling poverty in rural areas.

- helping rural businesses to succeed through improved skills, business support and better infrastructure (Chapters 7 and 8);
- helping farmers to restructure, become more competitive and consumer oriented and to develop speciality products, with reduced reliance on production subsidies, and reduced regulatory burdens and better advice and support;
- targeted support for deprived rural areas (Chapter 7);
- better rural services which combat poverty and social exclusion (Chapter 4);
- a planning system that encourages business growth, for example on farm diversification (Chapter 8) and provision of housing (Chapter 5) while meeting broad objectives to protect the rural environment;
- support to develop the potential of market towns for their economic role (including leisure and tourism) and as service centres.

Objective 2

To maintain and stimulate communities, and secure access to services which is equitable in all the circumstances, for those who live or work in the countryside.

- retain basic local services such as the Post Office (Chapter 3);
- provide modern rural services using ICT and flexible delivery (Chapter 4);
- more flexible and demand-responsive local transport (Chapter 6);
- increased provision of social and affordable housing in order to sustain balanced communities.

Objective 3

To conserve and enhance rural landscapes and the diversity and abundance of wildlife (including the habitats on which it depends).

- a vigorous and strong policy of protecting the countryside through redirecting new house-building pressure away from green-field sites and maintaining the quality of valued landscapes while meeting the needs of rural communities (Chapter 9);
- implementing a new direction for agriculture support which takes full account of the environmental benefits that farming provides (Chapter 10);
- a holistic approach for assessing landscape value (Chapter 9).

Objective 4

To increase opportunities for people to derive enjoyment from the countryside. To open up public access to mountain, moor, heath and down and registered common land by the end of 2005.

- increasing access to land as set out in the Countryside and Rights of Way Bill;
- improving the management and recreational potential of land on the urban fringe (Chapter 9).

Objective 5

To promote government responsiveness to rural communities through better cooperation between central departments, local government and government agencies and better cooperation with non-government bodies.

- a stronger role for town and parish councils that meet the Quality Test (improved consultation) and better recognition of rural issues in central and local government policy-making (Chapter 12);
- rural assessment of policy-making and implementation (Chapter 13).

Annex 2: Defra's aims, objectives and Public Service Agreements performance targets (2003–06) (Chapter 13 of the PSA White Paper accompanying the 2002 Spending Review)

Aim

Sustainable development, which means a better quality of life for everyone, now and for generations to come, including:

- a better environment at home and internationally, and sustainable use of natural resources;
- economic prosperity through sustainable farming, fishing, food, water and other industries that meet consumers' requirements; and
- thriving economies and communities in rural areas and a countryside for all to enjoy.

Objectives and performance targets

1. Promote sustainable development across government and the country as a whole as measured by achieving positive trends in the government's headline indicators of sustainable development.
Objective I: Protect and improve the rural, urban, marine and global environment, and lead integration of these with other policies across government and internationally.

2. Improve the environment and the sustainable use of natural resources, including through the use of energy-saving technologies, to help reduce greenhouse gas emissions by 12.5 per cent from 1990 levels and moving towards a 20 per cent reduction in carbon dioxide emissions by 2010.

3. Care for our natural heritage, make the countryside attractive and enjoyable for all, and preserve biological diversity by:

- reversing the long-term decline in the number of farm-land birds by 2020, as measured annually against underlying trends;

- bringing into favourable condition by 2010 95 per cent of all nationally important wildlife sites; and
- opening up public access to mountain, moor, heath and down and registered common land by the end of 2005.

Objective II: Enhance opportunity and tackle social exclusion in rural areas.

4. Reduce the gap in productivity between the least well-performing quartile of rural areas and the English median by 2006, and improve the accessibility of services for rural people.

Objective III: Promote a sustainable, competitive and safe food supply chain which meets consumers' requirements.

Objective IV: Promote sustainable, diverse, modern and adaptable farming through domestic and international actions.

5. Deliver more customer-focused, competitive and sustainable food and farming as measured by the increase in agriculture's gross value-added per person excluding support payments; and secure CAP reforms that reduce production-linked support, enabling enhanced EU funding for environmental conservation and rural development.

Objective V: Promote sustainable management and prudent use of natural resources domestically and internationally.

6. Enable 25 per cent of household waste to be recycled or composted by 2005/06.

7. Reduce fuel poverty among vulnerable households by improving the energy efficiency of 600,000 homes between 2001 and 2004.

Objective VI: Protect the public's interest in relation to environmental impacts and health, and ensure high standards of animal health and welfare.

8. Improve air quality by meeting our National Air Quality Strategy objectives for carbon monoxide, lead, nitrogen dioxide, particles, sulphur dioxide, benzene and 1-3 butadiene (joint target with DfT).

9. Protect public health and ensure high standards of animal welfare by reducing:

* the annual incidence of bovine spongiform encephalopathy (BSE) to less than 30 cases by 2006; and
* the time taken to clear up cases of poor welfare in farmed animals by 5 per cent by March 2004.

Value for money

10. Achieve a reduction of 10 per cent in the unit cost of administering CAP payments by 2004/05 and an increase to 95 per cent electronic service delivery capability for such payments by 31 March 2005.

PART II

MIGRATION, PLANNING AND TRANSPORT

3   IN-MIGRATION AND ITS IMPACTS ON THE RURAL ECONOMY

Aileen Stockdale[1]

Introduction

The movement of people from town to country has been a marked feature of internal migration flows in Western countries during recent decades (Berry, 1978; Blotevogel and Fielding, 1997; Rees et al., 1996), including the United Kingdom (Champion, 1989, 2000; Stillwell et al., 1992). Rural in-migration will inevitably have consequences for the host areas. These are of course likely to vary from one rural area to another and may be positive or negative. The tendency by many, however, has been to stereotype the consequences and, in doing so, blame in-migration for the many ills evident in rural communities. A few examples from recent academic research suffice to illustrate. Phillips (1998) refers to the colonisation of rural areas by professional and managerial service classes, Gilligan (1987) reports that in-migration raises local property prices, disadvantaging indigenous residents, and Simmons (1997) argues that incomers take jobs from locals.

These studies not only portray rural in-migration in negative terms but also ignore the wider rural restructuring that is taking

1   The author acknowledges the receipt of an award from the Countryside Agency for, and the contribution of Professor Allan Findlay (University of Dundee) to, the larger project from which this paper was prepared.

place. Cloke (1996) rightly asserts that 'the causes of rural change are recognised as occurring outside the rural area altogether' (p. 435). Examples include the restructuring of agriculture and the emergence of a diversified rural economy (Ilbery and Bowler, 1998), the development of housing and transport network policies that have made former remote locations attractive places of residence, and the increasing ability of individuals to fulfil their residential preferences.

Recognising the potential role of rural restructuring and broader economic and social changes permits a more objective assessment of the migration impacts, in particular allowing one to highlight the benefits as well as the problems. As long ago as 1990, Fielding asserted that rural in-migration 'must be seen as both a threat and a blessing' (1990: 238). Nevertheless, few works have highlighted the potential blessings. Exceptions include research by Cloke et al. (1997) in rural Wales and Findlay et al. (1999) and Stockdale et al. (2000) in rural Scotland.

This paper aims to take such a stance in relation to migration to rural England, focusing on its potential contribution to rural economic regeneration. This is assessed in relation to the job creation potential of in-migrants and their expenditure patterns. Within this context, it is worth bearing in mind that many rural areas are characterised by an ageing population (a legacy of prolonged periods of out-migration by the young), a narrow economic base (traditionally focused on the primary sector, which has undergone dramatic changes during the last century) and a rationalisation of rural services and facilities. It is essential therefore that this wider rural restructuring is considered when examining the economic impacts of migration.

Attempts to assess the impacts (economic or otherwise) of

in-migration are fraught with difficulty. In the absence of similar details regarding out-migration it is difficult to quantify the exact degree and nature of change. For example, there is no way of knowing whether incoming households are significantly different in character from out-going households. In addition, incoming households will have changed during the period since their move and rural restructuring and change will have affected all households.

The findings reported in this paper come from a much larger study (Findlay et al., 1999) relating to five study areas in England: Alnwick, Ashford (Kent), East Devon, South Warwickshire and the Wear Valley. Random household surveys were conducted in each area: 606 questionnaires were completed representing a 62 per cent response rate; 73 per cent (436 households) had moved to their current address since 1981 (hereafter termed migrants). Approximately half had moved no more than 15 kilometres to their current residence. Housing, employment and quality-of-life considerations were the main motivating factors behind the move. In-depth interviews were used to supplement the information obtained from the questionnaire survey.

The paper is organised into four parts. Part 1 reviews the economic characteristics of migrants to provide a context for an assessment of their impacts on the rural economy. Parts 2 and 3 relate to local labour market and expenditure impacts respectively. Part 4 offers a conclusion in which the policy implications of the findings are reported.

The economic characteristics of migrants

Two-thirds of migrant household heads were economically active (with 23 per cent retired[2]), thus contradicting the common misconception that retired people dominate migration into rural areas. Moreover, one in five were self-employed, offering the potential for job creation. This compares favourably with the proportion self-employed among the local population. Regional variations are, however, observed. The highest proportions of self-employed migrants were found in Alnwick (25 per cent) and South Warwickshire (23 per cent). The lowest proportion was in the Wear Valley (14 per cent). It is ironic that this older industrial area is arguably the study area that most needs job creation as a result of in-migration. Former industrial areas, however, find it difficult to attract small businesses because they do not match the quality-of-life criteria that attract entrepreneurial movers. Quality of life was the single most dominant reason for moving cited by self-employed migrants. Economically active migrants tend to work within 20 kilometres of their home (67 per cent): again contradicting the common misconception that in-migrants to rural areas are long-distance commuters to major towns and cities, and simply use the countryside as a dormitory.

Heads of migrant households generally command higher incomes than those of long-term households (30 vis-à-vis 13 per cent earn in excess of £25,000 per annum). Nevertheless, it is worth reporting that approximately one in five migrant heads of household earn less than £10,000 per annum. While this is significantly lower than the one in two among long-term household heads, the data do point to significant income variations within the migrant sample. This is explained by employment status, age and educational attainment differences.

2   This figure is strongly influenced by the dominance of retirement migration in the East Devon study area.

The labour market impacts of rural in-migration

The falling demand for agricultural labour was one of the key forces underpinning rural depopulation in England during the twentieth century. In recent decades agriculture, forestry and fishing have become ever less important sectors of rural employment while service sector jobs have grown in importance in both relative and absolute terms (Champion and Townsend, 1990). Of migrant heads of household in the sample (who were economically active), two-thirds were employed in the tertiary sector: predominantly in services/sales (23 per cent), banking and insurance (14 per cent), health and education (14 per cent), transport (8 per cent) and public administration (4 per cent). A minority (12 per cent) were involved in agriculture, forestry and fishing. Migration into rural England appears therefore to have strengthened the existing trend within the rural labour market away from primary production and into services. Importantly, few long-term residents (approximately 18 per cent) perceived that in-migrants take jobs from locals.

In-migration, however, has the potential to generate new jobs within the rural economy (Champion and Vandermotten, 1997). Whether this potential is realised will depend on the number of self-employed migrants and the capacity of their business for job creation (Findlay et al., 2000). Among the migrant heads of household in the survey, no less than 21 per cent (87 individual heads) defined themselves as self-employed. A further 28 adults living in migrant households defined themselves as self-employed on a full-time basis, with 13 in part-time self-employment. In total, the sample captured 128 self-employed adults (of which 26 were self-employed on a part-time basis) within migrant households.

It was often the case that migrants started businesses that did not employ many people; nevertheless, the potential generated by rural in-migration was recognised by many in the sample. The following quotes are illustrative:

> Well, the people next door, he's taken on a couple of units in Glanton, which I know have been standing empty for a long time. He's set up his own little business and he's actually employing one person locally. (Long-term resident in Alnwick)

> [I am a recruitment consultant for a software company.] It is actually a bloke who had worked in London but didn't need to sit in London to actually make software. ... He bought a farmhouse and set up one of the barns as an office and he is doing that as a job ... and has actually been expanding ever since. (Migrant in East Devon)

Among the self-employed migrant heads of household, some 86 per cent worked within their district of residence. Only 12 per cent based their business in a city or large town. Interestingly, 41 per cent had been full-time employees prior to their move.

> I work for myself now, got made redundant after they moved everyone up here [from London]. I now work from home for my own business. If I had stayed in London, I don't think I would have set up on my own. There is always so many jobs [in London], jobs with good perks ... [I] probably [would] just have gone along with that. (Migrant to South Warwickshire)

> I started off as a solicitor and my wife was a teacher. We got tired of working for other people. My wife is currently a driving instructor and I do editorial work on a freelance basis. ... A girl in one of the local villages works for me. ... (Migrant to Alnwick)

This suggests that migration to a rural area was part of their life goals in shifting to becoming self-employed, and that setting up a rural business was, in part, an outcome of the migration process. If a significant number of urban dwellers share the desire to move into self-employment at the same time as making an urban-to-rural residential shift, then this would be a feature meriting attention by regional policy-makers concerned to use migration as a tool to regenerate local economies. Several respondents, however, reported the lack or inaccessibility of appropriate schemes to encourage the establishment of a rural business.

> There was nothing specific for setting up here. I understand that in some areas they are quite keen on specific help to bring business in … I was told that there was nothing for this area … [I] didn't get any help to set up. (Migrant to South Warwickshire)

The extent to which self-employed migrants generated job creation in rural areas is evident from Table 5. Although 81 per cent employed no additional labour in their business, the remainder created a significant number of full-time jobs, especially the small number of businesses that employed five or more employees. Similar labour market impacts were noted by Findlay et al. (2000) in a Scottish sample of comparable size. In that study, however, some 45 per cent of self-employed migrants created jobs for others compared to only 19 per cent in England.

On average, for every self-employed migrant some 2.4 full-time jobs were created. The nature of the migrants' business influenced the potential for job creation. Each self-employed head of household working in the primary sector created on average 0.4 jobs. The corresponding number for those in the engineering and

Table 5 **Job creation by self-employed migrants**

Businesses with one or more full-time staff	Percentage	Number of full-time employees
No one other than migrant	81	0
1–4 employees	12	21
5 or more employees	7	223
Total	100	244

service sectors was 2.8 jobs. These findings are again in line with those of Findlay et al. (ibid.). Self-employed migrants also created part-time jobs for others (126 in total). These involved low-skill service tasks such as cleaning.

The number of jobs created by self-employed migrants may seem small on a national scale, but in the context of the sample size it represents a significant impact on rural labour markets. In addition to these totals service sector jobs generated by other migrant households (that is, non-self-employed migrant households) should be taken into account. Not surprisingly, only a minority of households headed by an employee (4 per cent) offered full-time work to anyone else. Much of the work generated was part-time, and in contrast to the high-quality service sector jobs associated with the majority of small businesses established by self-employed migrants, other migrants boosted demand in the rural economy for lower-skill, lower-wage jobs such as cleaning, gardening and childminding.

An increased demand for established rural businesses was also observed, most notably in the building sector. For example, in deciding to modify their rural homes migrants usually employed local tradesmen.

We made a conscious decision to try and find local material

so we used the joiner locally. We have used a furniture
maker almost within a mile of here. … That was a definite
decision to try and spend our money locally. I think if you
are sensitive to the people round about and you are sensitive
to the fact that a lot of them are working very hard and are
self-employed and are not finding it easy, then you try and
spend your money locally. (Migrant to Wear Valley)

The main hope for direct job creation in rural England comes
from the in-migration of self-employed people who bring their
businesses with them, rather than from the wider flow of migrant
households. Migration by the self-employed to rural areas brings
opportunities for significant employment expansion. This is not to
say that other migrants do not also contribute to economic growth
in rural labour markets, but the effects of this wider flow are likely
to be more evident in the increased demand for less skilled and
lower-paid service sector jobs.

Migrants' expenditure in the rural economy

It was noted above that migrants to rural areas generally earn
higher annual incomes than the local population. One important
consequence of this is that migrants are often accused of bidding
up house prices using their higher income levels (Gilligan, 1987;
Shucksmith, 1981). This can be counterbalanced by other forms
of expenditure. There is, for example, the possibility of higher-
income households spending more in local shops as well as
increasing demand for local services. It is place of work rather
than migration status, however, which is the most important
influence on income levels: 62 per cent of migrants who commute
over 20 kilometres earn in excess of £25,000 per annum compared

to 49 per cent who work locally. The stronger links maintained by migrant commuters with urban centres mean that only a small fraction of their expenditure ends up in the rural economy (Findlay et al., 2001).

Frequently purchased items (sundries, postal services) and perishable items (milk) were generally bought within the immediate area (Table 6). Larger and more valuable items (the weekly shop) were purchased in a neighbouring urban centre. This pattern was repeated among long-term residents. Thus migrants contribute no more or no less than long-term residents to the rural economy. The use of local provisions solely for low-cost or everyday needs means, however, that urban-based retailers are the main benefactors of rural in-migration. The numbers commuting to a city or large or small town, of whom 92 per cent purchase their weekly shopping beyond the immediate area, contribute to the loss of revenue from the rural area. The greater range and more competitively priced products available in urban centres make it virtually impossible for rural shopkeepers to compete.

> I use the [local] post office. The paper's delivered. The local shop we don't use that much, because I tend to do one large shop and that tends to see us through. (Migrant to Wear Valley)

Nevertheless, migrant households do their bit in helping to maintain at least a basic level of services within their immediate rural area (the local shop, where sundries and milk are purchased, post office, petrol station). The figure purchasing petrol locally would have been higher if it had not been for the closure of a petrol station in Rothbury (Alnwick) and the absence of such a facility in nearby villages. The closure of this petrol station has

Table 6 **Migrants' expenditure patterns**

	Immediate area	Neighbouring urban centre	Other urban centre	Total
Weekly shopping	29 (7%)	353 (91%)	8 (2%)	390
Milk	192 (49%)	191 (49%)	8 (2%)	391
Petrol	157 (42%)	200 (53%)	20 (5%)	377
Post office	246 (63%)	120 (31%)	24 (6%)	390
Bank	48 (12%)	310 (79%)	34 (9%)	392
Sundries	256 (69%)	110 (29%)	7 (2%)	373

led to increased expenditure in neighbouring towns. For example, since residents were required to travel to a neighbouring town for their petrol supplies they obtained other goods there at the same time. Equally important, the 7 per cent reliant on local retailers for their weekly shopping included low-income and older migrants. As such, it is not only local residents who experience the relative disadvantage associated with higher-priced rural retailers.

Conclusion

In common with many Western countries, England has participated in a process of population deconcentration. In-migration to rural areas is now an established trend. The characteristics of this trend are, however, variable between differing geographical areas, and are associated with varying impacts: some negative, others positive. Among the positive benefits are that in-migration provides an opportunity for economic regeneration. The job creation potential of self-employed migrants was found to be particularly important; on average, for every self-employed migrant some 2.4 additional full-time jobs were created. These were mainly in professional businesses, raising an issue as to the compatibility of local skills with the new job opportunities. Regional differences were also noted, with the Wear Valley in particular recording the lowest number of self-employed migrants. Non-self-employed migrants were also found to generate jobs for others within the local economy. While these were largely in low-paid service sector positions, such positions are nevertheless an important sector of the rural economy. In addition, in-migration may mean the difference between local services (for example, post office, village shop) remaining in rural areas or closing owing to falling demand. In broad terms in-migrants contributed just as strongly as long-term residents to rural service demand. Nevertheless, urban centres close to areas of in-migration often benefited most from increased demand; the failure by rural retailers to capture a greater share of household spending represents a significant loss of revenue from the rural economy.

This study confirmed that a number of self-employed migrants are attracted to rural areas by quality-of-life considerations. As such, policy initiatives addressing the quality-of-life perceptions of former industrial areas in particular should be incorporated into economic development strategies. Service providers on the whole need to be more aware of the potential spending power and investment potential of migrants. Rural regeneration may require migrants (and indeed the local population) to spend more of their income in the local economy; even a small increase in the fraction of income spent locally could make a significant contribution to the rural economy. Policy-makers also need to be mindful that the closure of one rural service or facility (for example, a petrol station) can adversely affect the shopping patterns associated with other products. Greater appreciation of the benefits that come from in-migration to rural areas may be an important first step on the road to rural regeneration.

References

Berry, B. J. L. (1978), 'The counterurbanisation process: how general?', in N. M. Hansen (ed.), *Human Settlement Systems*, Cambridge: Ballinger, pp. 25–49.

Blotevogel, H. and A. Fielding (1997), *People, Jobs and Mobility in the New Europe*, Chichester: Wiley.

Champion, A. (1989), *Counterurbanisation*, London: Edward Arnold.

Champion, A. (2000), 'Flight from the cities?', in R. Bate, R. Best and A. Holmans (eds), *On the Move: The housing consequences of migration*, York: Joseph Rowntree Foundation, ch. 2, pp. 10–19.

Champion, A. and A. Townsend (1990), *Contemporary Britain*, London: Edward Arnold.

Champion, A. and S. Vandermotten (1997), 'Migration, counterurbanisation and regional restructuring in Europe', in H. Blotevogel and A. Fielding (eds), *People, Jobs and Mobility in the New Europe*, Chichester: Wiley, pp. 69–90.

Cloke, P. (1996), 'Rural lifestyles: material opportunity, cultural experience, and how theory can undermine policy', *Economic Geography*, 72(4): 433–49.

Cloke, P., M. Goodwin and P. Milbourne (1997), *Rural Wales: Community and marginalisation*, Cardiff: University of Wales Press.

Fielding, A. (1990), 'Counterurbanisation and the characteristics: threat or blessing?', in D. Pinter (ed.), *Western Europe Challenge and Change*, London: Belhaven, pp. 226–39.

Findlay A., D. Short, A. Stockdale, A. Findlay, L. Li and L. Philip (1999), *Study of the Impact of Migration in Rural Scotland*, Edinburgh: Scottish Office Central Research Unit.

Findlay, A., D. Short and A. Stockdale (2000), 'The labour-market impacts of migration to rural areas', *Applied Geography*, 20: 333–48.

Findlay, A., A. Stockdale, A. Findlay and D. Short (2001), 'Mobility as a driver of change in rural Britain: an analysis of the links between migration, commuting and travel to shop patterns', *International Journal of Population Geography*, 7: 1–15.

Gilligan, J. (1987), 'Visitors, tourists and outsiders in a Cornish town', in M. Bouquet and M. Winter (eds), *Who from Their Labours Rest? Conflict and practice in rural tourism*, Aldershot: Avebury, pp. 65–82.

Ilbery, B. and I. Bowler (1998), 'From agricultural productivism to post-productivism', in B. Ilbery (ed.), *The Geography of Rural Change*, Harlow: Longman, pp. 57–84.

Phillips, M. (1998), 'Investigations of the British rural middle classes – Part 2: fragmentation, identity, morality and contestation', *Journal of Rural Studies*, 14(4): 427–43.

Rees, P., J. Stillwell, A. Convey and M. Kupiszewski (1996), *Population Migration in the European Union*, Chichester: Wiley.

Shucksmith, M. (1981), *No Homes for Locals?*, Aldershot: Gower.

Simmons, M. (1997), *Landscapes of Poverty: Aspects of rural England in the late 1990s*, London: Lemos and Crane.

Stillwell, J., P. Rees and P. Boden (1992), *Migration Processes and Patterns*, vol. 2, *Population Redistribution in the United Kingdom*, London: Belhaven.

Stockdale, A., A. Findlay and D. Short (2000), 'The repopulation of rural Scotland: opportunity and threat', *Journal of Rural Studies*, 16(2): 243–57.

4 'LOCALS-ONLY' HOUSING: THE MARCH OF THE NEW TOTALITARIANS?

John Meadowcroft

'Locals-only' housing describes restrictions imposed by local authorities and other government bodies on who can buy or own properties in particular localities. Rather than build 'social housing' for those deemed unable to meet their housing needs via the market – with the resultant problems of long-term housing management and ghettoisation of those on low incomes – local authorities are instead turning to direct intervention in the market for private houses with the aim of ensuring that those on low incomes can afford to buy properties in specific places. This involves preventing developers or home owners from selling their properties to certain categories of people.

A number of different 'locals-only' housing policies have been implemented in different places. In Gwynedd in Wales restrictions have been placed on the sale of former council houses, which can now only be sold to someone who has lived or worked within the local authority boundaries for at least three years. South Shropshire Country Council has granted planning permission to build new houses on the condition that they will be sold to people similarly deemed local. The Yorkshire Dales National Park Authority has likewise approved plans to restrict the sale of new properties within the park to people who have lived or worked in the area for three years.

Similar restrictions are being considered in other parts of

England, Wales and Scotland. Restrictions on who can own and rent property have existed in the Channel Islands since the immediate aftermath of World War II. While the constitutional and fiscal independence of the Channel Islands makes these restrictions inherently different, the results of 'housing controls' in the Channel Islands provide an important insight into some of the likely long-term consequences of 'locals-only' housing policies in other parts of the UK.

Supply and demand in the housing market

Prices in the marketplace are determined by supply and demand, so that where demand outstrips supply price will rise accordingly. The house price inflation that has occurred in many parts of the UK in the last decade results from the fact that there are insufficient houses to meet demand. The low supply of houses results from the UK's strict planning laws, which are weighted in favour of conservation and the 'nimby-esque' concerns of existing property owners, who are able to manipulate the planning system to thwart new development that might threaten the value of their property or the amenities that surround it. Such action is perhaps understandable given that the present system offers no provision for compensation for the loss of property values or local amenities that may result from development.

The demand for housing has risen as a result of long-term demographic trends that have been accelerated by low interest rates and the fact that for many decades property has been one of the best long-term investments in the UK, outperforming practically all the other options. High demand and low supply have fuelled house price inflation, though curiously 'locals-only' housing policies have not been implemented or even as yet proposed where house prices are highest – in Greater London and the South-East of England – but rather in rural areas where second-home owners, commuters and retirees are said to have pushed house prices beyond the level where they are affordable for many first-time buyers.

Problems created by excess demand can be solved either by increasing supply or by decreasing or rationing demand. To increase supply sufficiently to make a difference to house prices would require a relaxation of UK planning laws. Of course, there may be good reasons why the supply of houses in many areas should be limited – nobody wants to see areas of outstanding natural beauty built over with new housing – but the fact remains that a growing population cannot be housed unless new houses are built. The market signal coming loud and clear from the housing market is that a new balance has to be struck between conservation and development.[1]

'Locals-only' housing policies are an attempt to artificially lower demand so that it more closely corresponds with supply and hence prices fall. The theory is that demand for houses in a particular area can be reduced by introducing restrictions on who can buy those houses. To attempt to lower demand in this way, however, is ineffective and unfair.

---

1   Pennington (2000, 2002, 2005) and Corkindale (2004) have set out ways in which the UK's land-use planning system could be reformed so that market mechanisms allow a balance between development and conservation to be reached which would more accurately reflect people's needs and preferences.

Ineffectiveness of 'locals-only' housing policies

The principle of 'locals-only' housing is that by restricting demand to only those people who have lived or worked in a specific area for the past three years (or some alternative criteria) house prices will fall to a level within the reach of first-time buyers and other 'locals' presently priced out of the market. This policy assumes, however, that high demand is caused by 'incomers' rather than by a large number of 'local' people wishing to buy property.

The example of the Channel Islands is instructive here. Despite more than 50 years of 'locals-only' housing, the Channel Islands have not been exempt from the UK property price boom. In the last ten years house prices on the 'locals-only' market in Guernsey, for example, have more than trebled, so that the average house price rose from £90,000 in 1994 to £280,000 in 2004. Average local market house prices in the Channel Islands are markedly higher than in any other part of the UK, including Greater London.[2] Despite 50 years of 'locals-only' housing, the local markets of the Channel Islands are the most expensive places in the UK in which to purchase a property; if there is high demand for housing among 'local' people, then 'locals-only' restrictions will not bring about the desired reduction in house prices.

An unintended consequence of 'locals-only' housing may be the economic decline of those areas that adopt such policies. While the status of the Channel Islands as a tax haven for the super-rich (who may buy property on the 'open' market) has ensured their relative prosperity, 'locals-only' housing is frequently based upon a set of faulty assumptions about the economic impact of

---

2   In 2004, the Jersey average was £330,000 and the Guernsey average £280,000, compared to a UK average of £180,000, a Greater London average of £260,000 and a South-East England (excluding Greater London) average of £230,000.

commuter, retirement and holiday homes on rural areas. As Aileen Stockdale's chapter in this volume shows, retirees and commuters who live in the countryside tend to spend more money and hence bring greater economic prosperity than many long-term residents. Rather than turning rural areas into ghost villages, second-home owners, commuters and retirees bring much-needed economic sustenance. A locality that inhibits such inward migration will miss out on the economic benefits that follow.

Furthermore, 'locals-only' policies prevent locals themselves realising the true value of their house on sale. Preventing sale to the highest bidder is not only harmful to the seller, but is economically sub-optimal because the individual who values a house most highly is unable to purchase it. This may directly affect locals because their needs, and the prices they are willing to pay for the satisfaction of those needs, differ from the needs of incomers. For example, a small nineteenth-century cottage may well have a high value for a weekend summer dweller or as a holiday let but a much lower value for a permanent resident, who would be more affected by the poor standards of insulation, damp control, space availability, bathroom and kitchen facilities and so on. New developments of much cheaper houses, away from the picturesque centres of old towns, are frequently preferable for permanent residents. Hence, the sale of a home in a scenic village to a non-resident for a high price might well be a positive-sum game for all concerned.

Another unintended consequence of 'locals-only' policies may be cultural stagnation. Fifty years of housing controls have meant that the Channel Islands have been completely bypassed by many of the cultural changes that the rest of the UK has experienced. According to the 2001 census, non-white residents of Jersey, for example, constituted only 0.3 per cent of the population, compared to a UK average of 8 per cent. An unintended consequence of 'locals-only' housing policies may be the exclusion of ethnic minorities from particular areas and hence the creation of white-only enclaves.

Scarcity, liberty and 'locals-only' housing

In a free society scarce resources are rationed by the price mechanism rather than by political authority. That is, any individual may purchase a good or service so long as they are willing and able to pay for it. While this does mean that relatively well-off people will be able to consume more goods and services than the relatively less well off, it also means that no person is denied access to any good or service simply because they belong to a particular category of people. The prices generated in the marketplace provide information about the relative value of different goods and services, enabling people to pursue educational and employment opportunities that would allow them to purchase the goods and services they want. Hence, a person with a high preference for expensive sports cars, for example, should pursue a career that would enable them to buy a sports car or divert a large proportion of their income to such a purchase. By contrast, where goods and services are allocated by political authority a person with such a preference must seek to win political favour or lobby for the allocation of a sports car. Herein lies the difference between a free society where every individual has the liberty to pursue their own ends, and their success in so doing depends upon their ability to meet the needs of others in the marketplace, and an unfree society where political authority determines who gets what.

'Locals-only' housing policies mean that the allocation of

houses is determined, at least in part, by political authority. It compromises individual liberty and basic principles of fairness.

Is it fair that someone who has worked all their lives in order to buy a retirement home, or a second home, in an idyllic part of the country should be prevented from so doing so that another person can purchase a house in the same location at a lower price? On what basis is the 'local' person allowed to buy that house at a reduced price more deserving?

Is it fair that someone may be prevented from selling their house to an 'outsider' who wishes to buy it and must instead sell it for a lower price to another person? Why should that home owner be denied the market price for her home? Such a situation arose in Gwynedd in 2004, where a home owner was prohibited from selling the house that she and her late husband bought from the council more than twenty years previously to an English couple willing to pay £240,000 for it. Almost a year later, no alternative buyer for the house had been found.

By assuming that some people have a greater right than others to live in a particular location, 'locals-only' housing has the resonance of the 'no Irish' or 'no immigrants' policies employed in the 1950s by some landlords who wished to discriminate against particular races. Discrimination against outsiders, whether they be from another country or from another town, is generally regarded as immoral in a free society – to institutionalise such discrimination is surely wrong.[3]

---

3   It is worth adding that the discrimination by private landlords would probably not have been tenable had it not been for the Rent Acts restricting the supply of property.

Conclusion

This chapter has shown that 'locals-only' housing policies are unlikely to achieve their stated objectives. While one or two fortunate individuals may benefit from being allocated a property at a below-market rate, such policies are unlikely to fundamentally alter the mismatch between supply and demand in the housing market. This problem will be solved only by changing UK planning laws to enable a different balance to be struck between development and conservation. Abolishing stamp duty would also go some way to making home ownership more affordable for first-time buyers and others. Not only will 'locals-only' housing fail in practice, such policies are unfair and compromise the core principle of a free society that people are free to buy and sell their justly acquired property as they see fit.

In his 1944 classic *The Road to Serfdom* F. A. Hayek warned of the danger of a creeping totalitarianism that begins with the widespread acceptance that goods and services should be allocated by political authority rather than by the price mechanism and ends with the creation of a society based upon 'orders and prohibitions which must be obeyed and, in the last resort, the favour of the mighty' (p. 72). Hayek's critique of a planned economy in which production decisions are made by central authority may seem archaic today after the defeat of Nazism, the collapse of communism in Russia and eastern Europe and the abandonment of the post-war Keynesian consensus in most Western democracies, but a fundamental distrust of the market remains widespread in most liberal democracies. 'Locals-only' housing policies are an example of the way in which this distrust is being translated into public policy by a new generation of what Hayek termed 'the totalitarians in our midst'.

References

Corkindale, J. (2004), *The Land Use Planning System*, London: Institute of Economic Affairs.

Hayek, F. A. (1944), *The Road to Serfdom*, London: Routledge.

Pennington, M. (2000), *Planning and the Political Market*, London: Athlone.

Pennington, M. (2002), *Liberating the Land*, London: Institute of Economic Affairs.

Pennington, M. (2005), 'Competition for land-use planning: an agenda for the twenty-first century', in P. Booth (ed.), *Towards a Liberal Utopia?*, London: Institute of Economic Affairs.

5 THE POLITICISATION OF LAND-USE PLANNING IN THE COUNTRYSIDE
Chris Carter

Centralised control

The UK is unique among the world's major economies in the degree of control exercised by central government, which receives over 95 per cent of all taxation.[1] For the planning system, local government is effectively the delivery agent for central government planning policies that are maintained through legislation and regulations, national guidance statements, financial controls, targets,[2] performance indicators and a national inspectorate. Increasingly, however, local government is being overshadowed by the proliferation of quangos, development bodies and agencies that are being created to deliver national policy. The confluence of this hierarchical cascade of government tiers, government agencies and planning regulations is acting to create an increasingly politicised, bureaucratic, highly complex and burdensome system of land-use planning.

---

1   HM Treasury – total tax receipts 2002/03 £396.2 billion, of which: council tax £16.7 billion (4.22 per cent) and business rates £18.5 billion (4.67 per cent).
2   Cash for targets backfired recently as it encouraged abuse in the system whereby appeals to the Planning Inspectorate increased by 47 per cent because of unfair rejection of schemes by planning authorities to save time and meet targets ('Cash for targets linked to planning abuse', *Estates Gazette*, 21 August 2004).

The Sustainable Communities Plan

Driven by the deputy prime minister, John Prescott, MP, the government's response to the under-supply of housing and resultant house price inflation has been to produce the 'Communities Plan' to solve the housing shortage in the South-East of England and the phenomenon of housing abandonment in the North (ODPM, 2003). It sets out the government's plans to spend £22 billion on housing and communities to provide for a projected 200,000 homes in the South-East of England by 2016 in four earmarked growth areas,[3] which anti-development campaigners argue will 'concrete over the countryside'.

Although well intentioned, the plan's predict-and-provide approach replaces demand expressed by the price mechanism with forecasted need established by central government planners, and has been criticised as Stalinist, conjuring up fears of 1960s-style master planners concreting over green fields to create a meritocratic society. Notably absent from the plan, yet integral to its implementation, is a commitment from government departments, including the Treasury and the Department for Transport, to provide the infrastructure needed to service these new growth areas. The estimated cost for the South-East alone is £20 billion (£2 billion less than the Communities Plan budget). To date, the ODPM has committed only £610 million, but it appears to be pinning hopes on the introduction of a Planning Gain Supplement (PGS) to capture the uplift in value on land that has received planning permission,[4] and despite five failed attempts over the last

3   The ODPM has identified four growth areas: Milton Keynes South Midlands, the Cambridge–Stansted–Peterborough corridor, the Thames Gateway and Ashford.

4   *The Barker Report: Review of Housing Supply*, HM Treasury, 2004, recommended the introduction of a Planning Gain Supplement to capture some of the develop-

century, the government has been exploring turning this idea into a development land tax with the intention of funding infrastructure in growth areas. In cases of agricultural land being reclassified for commercial or residential use, this would mean large windfalls. It remains uncertain, however, whether a new form of development tariff will be hypothecated for the infrastructure it was designed to fund, and whether it will be collected and spent locally or centrally.

In order to deliver its growth plans, central government is presiding over the proliferation of a vast range of state-funded quangos, agencies and programmes. These include the creation of Regional Development Agencies (RDAs); Regional Housing Boards and Regional Planning Bodies;[5] development agencies such as English Partnerships; the Commission for Architecture and the Built Environment (CABE), a design watchdog; urban development corporations (UDCs);[6] and a plethora of programmes designed to tackle social exclusion, low housing demand, housing abandonment and wealth inequalities in deprived communities.[7] In addition to these programmes and agencies, central government also funds a large number of statutory agencies that play an integral role in the planning process.

ment gains that landowners benefit from, to fund social and transport infrastructure in the growth areas.

5   The ODPM is consulting on the merger of RHBs and RPBs, and the establishment of Regional Planning Executives to give independent advice on future housing numbers (*Housing and Planning in the Regions*, ODPM, November 2004).

6   The House of Commons ODPM Select Committee criticised the need for the establishment of two UDCs in the Thames Gateway. It said that it was 'not convinced that there is a need for more regeneration agencies' and that local authorities 'should manage the development process from the outset' (House of Commons Office of the Deputy Prime Minister Select Committee, 2003).

7   Programmes include: the Neighbourhood Renewal Unit, the Social Exclusion Unit, the New Deal for Communities and the Neighborhood Renewal Fund (ODPM, 2003: 21).

Out of the ODPM's £22 billion Communities Plan budget, these quangos and programmes, excluding the aforementioned statutory agencies, have already absorbed billions in public expenditure. The Local Government Association chairman argues that centralisation has neutered local authority innovation, flexibility and responsiveness, and with the increasing number of new initiatives, task groups, quangos and unelected, unaccountable agencies and regional bodies that span central government, these organisations now spend more than four times as much as local government (Lockhart, 2004). Owing to the sheer impossibility of coordinating such a complex web of quangos, agencies and programmes, combined with planning regulations that rival the tax code in complexity, the government risks creating layers of bureaucracy, the duplication of roles and responsibilities, and the further politicisation of the planning process.

The Planning and Compulsory Purchase Act 2004

Although the Planning Act 2004 was designed to speed up the planning system, it is likely to have the opposite intended effect. Under the rhetoric of modernisation and streamlining strategic planning, the new system retains, in a different form, the previous hierarchical planning framework. And unique to the UK legislative process, the vast majority of the provisions in the act are enabling measures that will be interpreted and set out in guidance by central government officials.

Rather than abolishing layers of planning controls, the reforms have been designed to consolidate central control via statutory Regional Planning Bodies (RPBs) that will replace the county-level planning bodies. RPBs will produce spatial plans for the regions, and local plans will be replaced by local development documents (LDDs).[8] This will shift strategic planning functions to the regional level as LDDs will be required to interpret these regional plans. Although regional planning bodies will be comprised of a consortium of elected local authority officials and members of representative groups, they have been criticised for a democratic deficit following the government's withdrawal of its devolution plans for the English regions.[9] It is unclear what proportion of these bodies will consist of directly elected members, but with regional control in the hands of a minority and the introduction of another layer of development plans, associated Statements of Community Involvement[10] and strategic environmental assessments, the new system will be a mixture of top-down pro-development policy with new layers of statutory plans competing against new platforms that may be exploited by highly mobilised special-interest anti-development coalitions 'to hijack the system'.[11]

For the development industry, the act has removed flexibility and certainty. In an attempt to bring forward the supply of housing permissions, the act reduces the duration of planning permission from five to three years and abolishes the ability of local authorities to grant extensions. Unfortunately for developers, this catch-all policy will affect all commercial development, which in many cases cannot begin within a three-year timescale owing to a number of

8   LDDs will replace local, unitary and structure plans.
9   In November 2004 the government lost its referendum for an elected regional assembly in the North-East of England and abandoned plans for a Regional Assemblies Bill.
10 It is a statutory duty under the Planning Act 2004 for local authorities to issue Statements of Community Involvement, which are frameworks for local communities to be consulted on LDDs.
11 'New guidelines will bring further delays to planning', *Estates Gazette*, 11 September 2004.

factors such as securing finance, brown-field land decontamination or receiving associated consents from statutory agencies.

Statutory agencies

Following the grant of planning permission, in most cases subsequent associated consents must be sought from statutory agencies, which include English Heritage (EH), English Nature (EN), the Highways Agency (HA), the Environment Agency (EA) and the water authorities, all of whom exercise a disproportionate amount of control over planning permission and whose objections can derail development.

The lack of incentive structures for new development results in agencies resisting developments that increase their workloads. The HA recently came under criticism from Royal Town Planning Institute past president Mike Haslam for causing unnecessary delays, and issuing knee-jerk 'holding' directions that halt development until a dispute is rectified. Haslam argued that the HA imposes unfeasible requirements for highways improvements to allocated sites, or may refuse development altogether. In more extreme cases the HA has been initially receptive to a development scheme but has issued a 'holding' direction, agreeing to withdraw the direction only after the developer agreed to fund off-site highway works. Haslam concluded that the HA should have its powers of direction removed, since its ability to direct the refusal of a planning application gives the HA too much power, and taking into consideration broader complaints about its practices, the HA's demands are precariously close to extortion.[12]

12 Royal Town Planning Institute president Mike Haslam sent an open letter to the ODPM on 21 January 2003.

Other statutory agencies, such as the Environment Agency and water authorities, must be consulted to provide associated consents, and it is routine for English Heritage to halt development for months or years by challenging planning permission.[13] Despite the heritage quango's record of blocking development, which runs counter to central government's pro-development agenda, the Department for Culture, Media and Sport's Designation Review is granting EH sweeping new powers.[14] The radical changes include EH taking direct control of the listing system from the government,[15] and the creation of a unified list of all historic sites and buildings, which could potentially enable EH to establish protection regimes over entire 'historic character areas' such as lands with ancient monuments, historic hedgerows or the sites of ancient battlefields. Another mooted change that would cement the conservation body's hold on the planning system is the proposed requirement for the establishment of statutory regional conservation bodies euphemistically named Sub-regional Resource Pools (SRRPs), which would make it a statutory duty for local authority planning departments to consult SRRPs on planning applications, thus adding another tier to the planning process and another hurdle to development. A further measure will see management agreements introduced between EH and owners of historic assets. These new responsibilities are likely to herald bureaucratic expan-

---

13   EH legal challenges have involved cases in London where it has objected to new developments obstructing views of St Paul's Cathedral, or joined anti-development campaign groups that successfully prevented the redevelopment of South Kensington Underground station.

14   DCMS Review of the Designation System, *Protecting Our Historic Environment: Making the system work better*, July 2003.

15   Previously, EH nominated sites and buildings for listing to be approved by the secretary of state. Now EH will have direct responsibility for the entire system.

sion, leading to calls for increased funding for the quango, whose £110 million annual government grant was frozen for 2005/06.

Although not currently a statutory consultee, the Commission for Architecture and the Built Environment (CABE) bears all the hallmarks of a statutory agency, and its growing influence in the planning process has been the subject of a review by the House of Commons ODPM Select Committee. Although CABE has no statutory role, its review of planning applications is fast becoming another stage in the planning process over which there is no mechanism for appeal, and its unelected, unaccountable design review boards have aroused much criticism.[16] Although it does not have statutory power to stop a scheme, CABE's opinion is being treated as definitive by local authorities, which can reject planning permission for projects worth millions.

This has created debate about the politicisation of design whereby CABE's preferences for one school of architecture could create an architectural orthodoxy over the objections of residents and democratically elected officials. As a quango, it relies on subjective judgements of value and aesthetic quality and bases its decisions on a system of nebulous criteria.[17] The 180-plus publications of this budget-maximising agency have been criticised for a lack of focus, leading to accusations that they are designed more for publicity than satisfying the demands of consumers by providing a comprehensive toolkit for architectural design. CABE has an annual budget of approximately £11 million, and comments on roughly 500 projects annually.

---

16   Mira Bar-Hillel's evidence to ODPM Select Committee in *The Role and Effectiveness of CABE*, *Fifth Report of Session, 2004–05*, HC 59, 9 March 2005.

17   CABE's ivory-tower subjectivism was exposed in 'Tacky and soulless? I quite warmed to it', Richard Morrison, *The Times*, 13 October 2004.

New regulations, thematic planning policy statements and powerful third-party groups

The planning system's original architects nationalised land use to prevent urban sprawl and preserve the fabric of towns and cities, but over the decades land-use planning has evolved into a highly complex web of micro-management whereby even the smallest change to a modest residential property requires state-sanctioned permission, and the centralisation of planning controls into one-size-fits-all, top-down national policies are unresponsive to local needs, while at the same time central and regional government planners have vast powers over national land-use policy, given the nature of secondary legislation, which makes them subject to political pressures and the targets of strong coalitions of anti-development campaigners.

Recent legislative change provided anti-development campaigners with opportunities to influence provisions in the Planning Act. Despite failing during the passage of the Planning Act to gain government support for third-party rights of appeal, Friends of the Earth (FoE) successfully campaigned for an amendment making planning permission a requirement for internal alterations to buildings, specifically mezzanines. As a testament to its power, the amendment gained all-party support in Parliament, and a general acceptance that out-of-town development is the primary cause of town centre decline.

FoE argued that the additional floor space created by mezzanine floors allowed traditional food retailers to expand into non-food retail space, which was detrimental to the vitality of town centre stores, and increased traffic levels, noise and disturbance.[18]

---

18   The Friends of the Earth briefing *How Supermarkets Avoid Planning Controls*, July 2003, outlined its proposals to close a major 'loophole' in existing planning law.

So successful was FoE that the ODPM minister stated that closing the 'loophole' would 'send the firmest possible signal to spivs in the retail industry ... who do not care about rebuilding our city centres ... and are hell bent on remaining out of town and will use anything they can to do it'.[19] The 'spivs' the minister referred to are large-scale UK retailers.

Of the 25 existing national thematic planning guidance documents, the controversial Planning Policy Statement 6 (PPS6) will determine the future of planning applications for out-of-town development and clarify the government's position. Current policy promotes the development of town centres and curtails out-of-town retail parks unless evidence can be provided of the retail need for a development in a particular location; the development can be accessed by public transport; and the developer can provide evidence that there are no suitable sites in town centres, even if it means the disaggregation of a store.

Following revision of PPG6 in 1993, which ushered in the presumption in favour of town centre development, the anti-development lobby has built on this to convince politicians that out-of-town development is the primary cause of town centre decline. Economic growth is considered to be static and town centres unable to adapt to out-of-town competition. The revised PPG6, now PPS6, reached the front page of the *Daily Telegraph*, known for its sympathies to amenity groups such as the Council for the Preservation of Rural England (CPRE). The cause of concern was loose wording in PPS6 allegedly sanctioned by the Treasury, which would relax the ban on out-of-town development. Notably, the CPRE stated that policies that opened a window to

---

19   Lord Jeff Rooker, Minister of State for Regeneration, House of Lords Hansard, 5 February 2004, col. 854 .

out-of-town development would have 'devastating effects' on the vitality of town centres. Research disproves these widely held beliefs, yet central government planners fail to recognise the damaging impact town centre protectionism and the lack of retail space have on the price of goods, which is the primary cause of the so-called 'Rip-off Britain'.[20]

Linked to the PPS6 debate, PPS7, *Sustainable Development in Rural Areas*, sets out development regulations for the country-side. PPS7 is highly prescriptive in that it discourages out-of-town development and advises local authorities to 'strictly' control development away from existing settlements. Both residential and commercial developments are subject to a vast array of regula-tions, and only those that are accessible by public transport are permitted. Local development plans must 'support development that delivers diverse and sustainable *farming* enterprises',[21] and the redevelopment and reuse of buildings must take account of a list of vague criteria interpreted by local authority officials. PPS7 is a blanket policy for the countryside which does not leave room for local conditions that could benefit from development that falls outside central government prescription. The environmental and sustainability criteria that are a precondition of planning permis-sion fail to consider less damaging uses such as small-scale housing that would reduce the pressure for intensification of agricultural land and meet growing demand, especially among the rural popu-lation (Pennington, 2002).

So-called 'affordable' housing policies have become inextri-cably linked with planning gain and are fast becoming another

---

20   McKinsey Global Institute, *Driving Productivity and Growth in the UK Economy*, 1998.

21   PPS7, *Sustainable Development in Rural Areas*, ODPM, p. 12.

prerequisite for planning permission. The government's *Planning Policy Guidance 3 (PPG3) Housing* is undergoing revision, along with Circular 1/97, the guidance document for S106 'planning gain' from the 1990 Planning Act. Planning gain as originally defined in the act was intended to mitigate the impact of a development, but planning gain is increasingly unrelated to development, with local authorities stipulating the provision of community facilities such as swimming pools, crèches, community centres or simply cash payments for 'local authority services' in return for planning permission, making planning gain indistinguishable from a tax for planning permission.[22]

Planning obligations are also used to secure the inclusion of an element of affordable housing in a residential or mixed-use development where there is a residential component. National guidance states that local authorities must identify the need for affordable or social housing and must set site-size thresholds above which the provision of a specified proportion of affordable housing would be expected. In London, the populist mayor Ken Livingstone has 'recommended' in his spatial development plan, known as the 'London Plan', that 50 per cent of all new housing development be allocated as affordable, of which 35 per cent should be social-rented and 15 per cent 'intermediate', including shared-equity or below-market-rent. In some cases, however, a financial contribution may be requested. The result of these affordable housing policies pushes up the price of the percentage of market housing

---

22 The potential for corruption within the system of negotiating S106 agreements was exemplified in *Private Eye*'s 'Rotten Boroughs' column of November 2004, which exposed Lambeth councillor Darren Sanders's e-mail correspondence with a colleague, wherein he stated that 'it may be prudent to look at any potential planning applications … and see if S106 (planning gain/bribes) is [sic] useful …'.

on developments beyond the range of those on modest incomes, which creates a vicious circle of an artificial reliance on the state to allocate, as it wishes, the remaining percentage of a developer's housing as affordable units. The London Plan is the first Regional Spatial Strategy to be published, and is likely to set a precedent for future regional plans nationally.

The new localism

Central government prescription fails to take into account local circumstances, and the nature of local government finance has created in-built disincentives for development in the UK. Under the current system, developers must confront a mass of bureaucracy, regulations, special interests, quangos, statutory agencies and burdensome costs to drive forward growth. This is not a successful formula for countryside development or the regeneration of Britain's towns and cities, and any development that does occur over the course of the next decade will happen *despite* the planning system.

The chorus of calls for decentralisation is growing louder, and localism has captured the Zeitgeist, with numerous reports calling for greater local authority autonomy (for example, Carswell, 2004; Local Government Association, 2004; McFarquhar, 1999; Travers, 2003). Although localism will not be a panacea for the problems associated with development, it is the case that mass decentralisation, the devolution of tax-raising powers and of planning controls to local authorities would herald the beginning of a renaissance in Britain. With the removal of central government's monopoly of control on taxation and planning, and its micro-management of public services, the advent of locally raised finance would incentivise local authorities to encourage economic growth through development in order to increase tax revenue to fund local services.

Although the devolution of planning controls to the local level may increase a tendency towards nimbyism in some areas, the advent of the Tiebout effect (Tiebout, 1956; Pennington, 2002: 70–71) would mean that a highly mobile population would force authorities to compete for residents or face the threat of lost population and lost tax revenue. This would increase local democratic accountability and restore the link between local economic development and the provision of local services, while removing the dead hand of central control. Alas, since the last major legislative change occurred more than a decade ago, and the new planning reforms are likely to be in place for some time to come, the system will continue to limp along, curtailing dynamism and promoting mediocrity until a new wave of reformers take the mantle.

References

Carswell, D. (2004), *Paying for Localism*, London: Adam Smith Institute.

HM Treasury (2004), *The Barker Report: Review of housing supply*, London: Stationery Office.

House of Commons Office of the Deputy Prime Minister Select Committee (2003), *Empty Homes and Low Demand Pathfinders*, London: Stationery Office.

Local Government Association (2004), *Independence, Opportunity, Trust – A manifesto for local communities*, London: Local Government Association.

Lockhart, S. B. (2004), 'Core communities', *Parliamentary Brief*, October, p. 29.

McFarquhar, A. (1999), *Planning Rape*, London: Adam Smith Institute.

ODPM (Office of the Deputy Prime Minister) (2003), *Sustainable Communities: Building for the future*, London: Stationery Office.

Pennington, M. (2002), *Liberating the Land*, London: Institute of Economic Affairs.

Tiebout, C. (1956), 'A pure theory of local expenditures', *Journal of Political Economy*, 64: 416–24.

Travers, T. (2003), *Decline and Fall of Local Democracy*, London: Policy Exchange.

6 TRANSPORT AND THE COUNTRYSIDE
John Hibbs

Demand and supply

The growth of market towns starting in the eleventh century led to the need for regular and reliable transport, to bring goods and people in from the villages and to take them back. Field roads appeared, as the carriers made their way, a trade that lasted for almost a thousand years, and can still be traced in some of the rural bus services of today. Movement over longer distances was limited to the wealthy or the military, and became more general only after the Tudor Settlement, with stagecoaches appearing in the 1600s. Rural transport remained more important than urban transport until towns and cities started to grow in the eighteenth century.

The stagecoaches were local as well as national, linking neighbouring towns and serving villages on the way. Goods and agricultural products moved by road in growing quantities and over long distances as well as short, with poorer people as passengers. When the railways came use of the stagecoaches diminished, but some remained on local routes and developed into horse-drawn bus services. Freight movement by road continued and grew. Rural railways and branch lines spread in the latter part of the nineteenth century, with some pressure from government to cross-subsidise them from the main-line services. Light railways never developed to the same extent they did in France. In East Anglia the Great Eastern Railway opened several 'farmer's lines' prior to World War I, but their profitability was always in doubt.

In the countryside the impact of motor vehicles was far greater than the impact of steam had been a century before. The carriers' carts were replaced with buses, while the distribution of goods moved to vans. The buses were generally more convenient than the railway stations, while motor vehicles could carry fruit and vegetables directly to market, without the need to use the train. At the same time, starting before 1914, larger bus companies began to appear, providing services over wide areas and negotiating mutual boundary agreements to form a national cartel. In addition to the market-day services, a regular pattern of inter-urban bus routes was established everywhere, except in the most remote parts of the countryside.

By 1930 there had appeared a network of express coach services (outwith Scotland), which flourished because they were cheaper than the trains. Subject to state-controlled standard mileage rates, railway cross-subsidy grew as demand for many train services fell, keeping long-distance train fares unnecessarily high. The 1930s saw the four main-line railway companies in financial trouble, but very few lines were closed. The Road Traffic Act of 1930 gave bus operators monopoly rights on their licensed routes, and one result was consolidation of ownership, as smaller firms took advantage of this and sold to the cartel.

The bus services were well loaded until car ownership started to grow at the end of the 1950s. From then on decay set in, but fares were controlled on a standard rate per mile by the traffic commissioners, and the larger companies failed to understand their costs. By comparing average revenue per mile with average cost per mile, they cut services that were making a contribution to overheads, and so increased the burden of fixed costs – whereupon they cut some more. Some of the state-owned companies obtained authority to charge a higher rate per mile on their rural bus services, which made matters worse, after which they tended to withdraw from 'deep rural' areas. Only the small firms with lower overhead costs managed to keep their services going.

The problem was quickly recognised, and a *Report on Rural Bus Services* (the Jack Report) appeared in 1961. As with similar studies of the Highlands and Islands and by the Council for Wales and Monmouthshire, the conclusion was that the only continuing solution was direct subsidy in individual cases. Apart from the remission of fuel tax for bus mileage, nothing was done to provide for this, and cross-subsidy from urban operation was seen to be the answer. Two years later the Beeching Report identified similar problems for rural railways, but this time the answer was to close them.

The relationship between demand and supply continued to change. First the railways had lost traffic to the buses and then both industries felt the impact of private motoring, while the railways lost their freight traffic to road haulage and distribution. The Smeed Report of 1964 might have led to a more rational charging system for roads, to the advantage of the railway, but nothing was done. The great weakness of transport policy has always been the desire to look at railways or buses or lorries, but never at the market for *movement*, whether of people or goods. And the car has become the biggest player in the passenger market because it can offer what people most want: door-to-door movement.

How it has gone

The movement of both passengers and goods in the country-side today is overwhelmingly by road. Scattered settlements and small towns cannot generate enough demand for bus services on the urban model, which is dependent upon the first choice of the consumer, for frequency. For 25 years after 1945 the pattern of rural bus services depended upon the out-and-home market day and Saturday trips, strengthened over some links to a daily service, often supported by children attending secondary schools in the towns. Employment was local, predominantly in agriculture, and commuting to work was almost unknown. Services between towns had an attractor at each end, which balanced demand in a way that traditional rural services could not achieve, but when firms based in the villages sold to cartel companies it often meant twice the mileage, with empty journeys to start and finish. Much depended upon the actual siting of each village, those on a main road having a clear advantage, but around 1960 most villages had a bus service at least once a week, and in some cases two or more, offering access to more than one town.

The private car and the seismic shift in agricultural employ-ment changed all this. At first it was middle-class passengers who deserted the bus, as the car made it so much easier to carry the week's shopping home. But the 1960s saw the beginning of a continuing social change, as farming jobs disappeared, and men had to look for work away from the village. The expansion of car ownership across the working class, which has been such a marked feature of the past 50 years, started as a necessity in the countryside, so that men could drive to work, but a consequence was that the car would be available for shopping, in the evening and on Saturdays and the 'picture bus' rapidly disappeared.

Finally the car made it possible for people to move into the villages from the towns, either commuting or working for service industries. The more remote the settlement the greater the importance of the private car. In the 1970s the county of Radnorshire, for example, had the highest level of car ownership in Britain. Holiday travel and family visits were made easier, and the railways and express coaches lost traffic as well. Movement patterns that had developed over a millennium changed almost out of recognition. Whereas the car was once a supplement to public transport, today it is the other way round.

In the same way the distribution of goods and foodstuffs has passed entirely to road transport. As well as the Post Office and its competitors, there are networks of parcels movement that cover the whole country, offering guaranteed overnight delivery and linking with Continental and overseas networks as well. Goods are collected from any address and delivered to any other by a process that makes up loads at urban warehouses, whence they are carried by trucks on the 'stem movement' to hubs in the Midlands, where they are re-sorted and forwarded to the provincial centres or abroad. In the countryside the collection and delivery are by van or private car, and by this process there is a reliable link from every address to any other. Village shops are serviced in the same way through hubs organised by the retail trade, while similar networks supply the needs of the building trade and those who maintain the properties. Telephones and the Internet mean that people living in the countryside have as easy an access to their desires as anyone living in a city or town.

The way things are

Public transport – trains and buses – can be seen to be marginal in the countryside today. The Beeching plan, which rescued the main lines from incipient decay, depended upon fast inter-city services, and intermediate stations had to be closed. Rail freight has similarly been concentrated on trunk movement, and village goods stations and sidings have long since disappeared. Railway stations are few and far between, and the bus comes much closer to people's doors than the train ever did. Train lovers still promote the rural lines that remain, and seek to reopen some that have been closed, but it is difficult to justify public expenditure for what is perhaps best seen as a hobby. Where lines are operated by volunteer workers a service can be provided, but it cannot be seen to be essential, and many run simply when there is demand from visitors. People living in the countryside and in the small towns contribute through taxation to the cost of the railway, but they make hardly any use of it.

The central transport problem for people in the countryside today is the cost of motoring. This turns on two things: taxation and the price of fuel. While these are linked because of the sumptuary taxation of fuel, there is a specific issue concerning the economics of supply. Petrol prices at the pump vary widely according to levels of demand, so that they are cheaper where there is concentrated demand. There are few filling stations in rural areas in any case, but the outcome is that fuel is more expensive in just the areas where cars are most important.

Little can be done about the price of petrol, before tax. The combination of distance for deliveries and limited demand makes for a problem that will not go away, and one that exists in small towns as well as in the villages. Taxation, though, is another matter. The combination of car tax, vehicle excise duty and VAT, in addition to the fuel tax, produces revenue for HM Treasury far in excess of the expenditure on the roads: in 1999 road users paid a surplus of some £26 billion to government, over and above the total road expenditure (Mumford, 2000). This excess is much greater per mile in towns and cities than it is in the countryside. That apart, it has been shown (ibid.) that rural road users pay some seven times too much in terms of excess taxation when compared with the social costs they create, which are far less than in the cities, where costs of congestion and pollution are greater. The obvious solution to this is road-use pricing that varies with congestion, combined with a suitable reduction in vehicle excise duty and fuel tax.

What, then, would be the consequences for public transport operators? When I looked at the problem in 1970 (Hibbs, 1972) I considered this. I said: 'If then the car is so much better than the train or bus for rural transport, what is the problem? Why not let things take their course? Surely there is no merit in supporting an obsolete system?'

In the long run I suspect that these objections are in fact valid; but we have, to some extent at any rate, a transitional problem, and a requirement that we should ease any transitional hardship. What has happened since then has been the progressive reduction of rural bus services, offset to some extent by the provision of coach services on contract for children, as the village schools have disappeared, along with the shrinking population. The industry as I described it in the 1980s (Hibbs, 1986: ch. 7) has not changed a great deal, except for the intervention of well-meaning local authorities.

In the 1960s Devon County Council, recognising the rural

transport problems of its area, took the lead by encouraging the development of new services, small sums of money being made available for publicity. Under the Transport Act of 1968 the post of Transport Co-ordinating Officer (TCO) was made mandatory at county council level and the use of direct subsidy was for the first time permitted. The act, however, contained no provision for defining 'public need', and the extent to which intervention took place varied considerably from one county to another. After 1972 the metropolitan counties (which contained considerable areas of countryside) as Passenger Transport Authorities invited the Chartered Institute of Public Finance and Accountancy (CIPFA) to develop a technique for allocating subsidy, but this proved to be of little value. In the event the TCOs were faced with a conflict, between 'fire-fighting' reaction when a firm gave the required notice of withdrawal of a service and some attempt at the 'nurturing' of new services perceived for some reason to be desirable.

It cannot be said that the intervention and use of subsidy since 1968 have been above reproach in terms of value for money, or in the maintenance of such services as people in the countryside still need. TCOs have been accused of seeking to act as 'virtual bus managers' while some have been seen to be bus enthusiasts, detached from economic reality. Some councils have required buses used on subsidised services to carry a specified livery, and appear to have been attracted by the idea of running the buses themselves. The outcome has been a pattern of confusion; empty buses on some routes ('buses carrying fresh air') and little or no change on others. Where TCOs have invented new services the result has sometimes been the withdrawal of marginally profitable services operated commercially by private firms. Policy in some counties has swung from one extreme to another after changes in political control, and drastic cuts have been made when the cost of subsidy has become too great. Neither should it be forgotten that the small firms provide a mix of public and private services as well as school transport, so that the withdrawal of subsidy can disturb the prosperity of the business.

What can be done?

Two aspects of the rural transport problem need to be faced if a more satisfactory solution is to be found. Both are related to the nature of local government. We have a case here of a degree of market failure followed by the failure of government intervention – a classic example of public choice theory at work. Then this has been worsened by the cultural gap arising from the urban location of the local authority, and in some cases by the establishment of unitary authorities, and complicated by the vote motive. It is difficult for an official in a town, under the pressures of the job, to have the detailed information and 'feel' for the situation in villages that may be many miles away, and any attempt to second-guess the market can only tend to worsen the situation. The loss of a school contract by a local firm can undermine the viability of a deep rural service, which means that inter-departmental barriers should not be allowed to get in the way of sensible solutions.

This is not to say that some degree of subsidy may not be desirable in the countryside. With the availability of the car being more general today, there is now a minority demand for bus (and train) travel, from older people and those without a car (as well as for children to get to school). The number of people concerned varies considerably from area to area and is best judged by those who live there. For this purpose it may be helpful to distinguish broadly between *suburban rural* and *deep rural* areas, while allowing for an uncertain boundary between the two.

Suburban rural areas surround the cities and larger towns, and at their most extreme they contain villages that have departed completely from the traditional pattern. Within car commuting distance of Norwich, for example, there are villages where virtually no one is around during the day, other than at weekends; where there is no school, no post office and no pub, while the Anglican parish priest will be responsible for half a dozen such communities. These examples may be extreme cases of the phenomenon, but the urbanisation of the countryside has been a result of car ownership and its consequences, in broader social terms, have been severe. Villages of this kind simply do not need public transport.

In the deep rural areas there has been less change from the traditional pattern, and some villages may still have the same sort of bus service as was usual 30 years ago, although demand will have fallen over the years, most markedly on Saturdays, once the busiest day of the week. Public transport here will vary from place to place, with villages on main roads getting a better bus service than others, but the market for movement is there, and bus companies large or small must be able to compete with the car for their share of it. There have indeed been examples of good marketing, targeting individual villages or redesigning inter-urban services. Recently the regulations have been eased, to allow diversions to be made in response to telephone requests.

Sound costing, especially recognising escapable costs, and readiness to experiment with prices can encourage demand, but there is also the need to improve the perceived status of the bus, which has not been helped by the attitude of planners in the market towns, where all too often the bus stands have been moved off the streets, while multi-storey car parks give immediate access to the shops and pedestrianisation has made things worse for bus passengers. Lessons could be learned from the retail trade, with promotion by leaflet to every door in the area of a service.

A practical suggestion

No one knows the requirements of deep rural villages better than those who live in them. The problem can be tackled at this level in two ways, bringing the decisions to where they belong. The first thing is to give parish councils power to raise a local rate, if they think fit, to provide a subsidy to bus operators; alternatively they could apply to the council concerned for the money. It might be best for neighbouring parishes to work together for this purpose. By bringing the finances to this level there should be less risk of waste, with buses carrying fresh air. For this to work a second provision would be desirable, bringing local people and bus operators together from time to time to look at the way the services are working. I arranged such a meeting in North Devon some years ago and all who took part found it most useful. The bus people learned about local needs and welcomed new ideas, while making suggestions themselves. They also explained in some cases why they would not be able to take the new work on. The Transport Co-ordinating Officer should attend such meetings and act as an 'honest broker', while obtaining advance notice from operators who could forecast the need to alter a service or to close it down. But the less the district council or unitary authority or for that matter the area traffic commissioner had to do with the process the better.

But road pricing itself would have substantial benefits. Glaister and Graham (2004) have shown that traffic in many rural areas would increase by about 25 per cent if a fully efficient set of road prices were charged throughout the country. As has been noted, road prices would be lower in rural than in urban areas. This increase in road use reflects much lower charges than the charges implicit in the current set of road taxes (which would be abolished). Given the extent of car use and the significant capacity of rural roads to carry more traffic, this would represent a considerable benefit to rural communities, even if there were no increase in public transport provision.

References

Glaister, S. and D. Graham (2004), *Pricing Our Roads*, London: Institute of Economic Affairs.

Hibbs, J. (1972), 'Maintaining transport services in rural areas', *Journal of Transport Economics and Policy*, 6(2).

Hibbs, J. (1986), *The Country Bus*, Newton Abbot: David & Charles.

Mumford, P. (2000), *The Road from Inequity – Fairer ways of paying the true costs of road use*, London: Adam Smith Institute.

7   RURAL RAIL
Paul Withrington

Introduction

The road system in most rural areas consists of a collection of tarmacked cow trails sometime doubling as 'A' roads, principal or trunk. These roads have unpredictable alignments with steep hills and wend their way through town and village alike – serving pedestrians, cattle and tractors along with motor traffic. Rural railways overlay this network. The rights of way are superbly engineered, offering excellent horizontal alignments and nearly flat vertical ones. They bypass small settlements and provide access to the hearts of larger ones. Everywhere they are segregated from cattle, tractors and pedestrians. The traffic carried on each element of this network is equivalent to, at most, a couple of half-full buses once an hour. The great majority of these routes were built with private money with the expectation of making a profit on the investment.

Where the (rail) routes are double-track or on double-track formation the level width is typically 8.5 metres, narrowing to 7.3 metres at bridges and tunnels. 7.3 metres is the carriageway width required for a two-way trunk road. Single-track lines can often be widened at modest cost to provide at least a 6-metre carriageway. Despite this, few of these routes have been converted to roads. Instead, abandoned lines have often been broken up or given over to rabbits, hedgehogs and cyclists. This paper outlines some of the history and asks the question: Why?

Beeching

Prior to the Beeching Report (British Railways Board, 1963) the annual operating subsidy for the national railways at 2004 prices was running at some £1.2 billion. Beeching pointed out that on half the network the trains did not cover the track costs and that at half the stations costs were greater than passenger receipts. He believed that if the uneconomic elements were removed the remainder would be financially viable. At the time there were 22,000 route miles in Great Britain's rail network, made up as shown in Table 7.

Table 7 **Route miles of Britain's rail network pre-Beeching**

	Open to passengers	Freight only
4 tracks and over	1,500	100
3 tracks	400	100
Double-track	10,000	1,200
Single-track	5,900	2,700
Total	17,800	4,100
Grand total	21,900	

The record does not provide the proportion of single track built on double-track formation, but often that was the case.

Following the Beeching cuts and over the subsequent decades the network's length has been reduced to 10,000 miles. At great loss to the nation, little or no attempt was made to preserve the abandoned 12,000 miles. Consequently almost all has been lost to transport use. The reasons for this tragic failure include:

1   The Railway Acts. These forced British Railways to sell land
    to the highest bidder. Hence, where lines entered urban areas
    the price offered by developers was generally above the price
    that a highway authority would pay.
2   The determination of railway enthusiasts that if a railway
    could not be preserved as a railway it should be abandoned.
    Indeed, more than 35 years ago a permanent under-secretary
    told his minister that one could not make a road from a
    railway: it was 'too straight' and 'too level' (Dalgleish, 1982).
3   A mistaken belief that railways are too narrow to be
    converted to roads. The latter is patently untrue: see below.
4   The environmental impact of bringing a substantially
    disused railway into effective transport use – overlooking
    the environmental benefits that such a road might bring by
    removing traffic from unsuitable rural roads, villages and
    towns and avoiding the need to build other roads.
5   Rural routes often terminated at main lines, so denying access
    to the ultimate destinations.

Consequently route integrity was lost, even on major routes such as the Great Central Line connecting Marylebone to Leicester.

Today, in contradiction to Dr Beeching's belief and despite his cuts, rail's annual operating subsidy has the long-run average of £2.5 billion. When capital is added the subsidy for the current decade has the range £(4.5–6.5) billion annually.

Transport Committee inquiries and Community Rail

Against that background the Transport Committee of the House of Commons held an inquiry into the future of the railways in 2003/04 and into rural rail in 2004. The key questions set out in the press notice prior to the former were:

- Is the regulator right, or is rail an outmoded form of transport?
- Is the present network the right one; if not, how should it be changed?
- What sort of traffic is the network best suited for?
- How does our network compare with other railways?

Instead of dealing with the fundamentals called for by its own brief, the committee became convinced that it was the management structure which needed changing. Hence its report (House of Commons Select Committee 2004) is a fine exposure of the confusion generated by the four parties involved – namely, the government itself, the Strategic Rail Authority, the Office of the Rail Regulator, and the network manager, Network Rail.

The inquiry into rural rail was preceded by the Strategic Rail Authority's consultation document on 'community rail' (Strategic Rail Authority, 2004a). Despite the fact that it runs to 29 pages, virtually the only hard facts provided are that the network contains '1,300 route miles or 12.5% of the national network and includes 420 stations (17% of the total)'. Instead of reasoned argument the thread that runs through the document is that government has decreed *ipso facto* that rail is a 'good thing' – so the 'need' for railways cannot be challenged. The two quotes below (from page 2 of the Consultation document) and associated comment following illustrate.

Quote: The Railway is fulfilling a new role, never envisaged 30 years ago, in terms of tackling local traffic congestion, or as part of the tourist economy or in providing environmentally friendly access to the historic coastal towns and national parks.

Comment: (a) The impact of rural rail on (negligible) local traffic congestion will be vanishingly small. (b) The tourist economy would benefit far more if the immense subsidy paid to rail were available directly to the tourist economy. Better still, for the nation as a whole, if the tax had been left in private hands, leaving the market to decide its best use. (c) Rail uses nearly double the fuel per passenger-mile required by express coaches (Transport-Watch, 2004).

Quote: The Gap between cost and income on these lines reflects the high fixed cost of providing a rail service ... Nevertheless, neither closure nor further conventional cost cutting can resolve the issue. Closure of railway infrastructure is not part of Government Policy nor the Secretary of State's Directions and Guidance to the SRA ... So, there is an overwhelming need to break out of this circle, to reduce the gap between income and cost and to increase the value of the railway to the community measured in terms of financial support per passenger journey.

Comment: These convoluted paragraphs mean that we (the SRA) are going to change nothing and cannot influence government policy. Hence rural rail needs more (lots more) money from the taxpayer.

In November, following the consultation exercise, the SRA

published its Community Rail Development strategy (Strategic Rail Authority 2004b). It provides slightly more data than the consultation document, namely:

1   The network length is now 1,200 miles.
2   Annual infrastructure costs are £100,000 per track-mile – including station renewal.
3   Rolling-stock costs for leasing and heavy maintenance are £100,000 per year per vehicle, representing 50–75 per cent of total vehicle costs.
4   Government cash support for the rail industry ran to £2.6 billion in 2002/03.
5   Subsidy to Community Rail costs approximately £300 million per annum.

That is substantially it: there is no estimate of passenger or freight usage; there is no schedule of the track lengths for the routes provided in the appendices; the SRA has no idea of the proportion of the network that has double-track formation, i.e. the widths (instead, if asked, it provides the general enquiry number at Network Rail, which is quite helpless). Likewise there is no comparative data for the adjacent road network.

Against that background the SRA quote the Institute of Chartered Accountants as finding that three-quarters of its members believe that local rail is important to the business economy of their region. How any person could come to any conclusion, let alone that one, in the absence of data remains a mystery. This chapter will now provide estimates of some of the blanks.

Flows

Although this information is not included in the publications, the SRA will say that the 1,300 miles of the Community Rail network carry 23.6 million passenger-journeys per year. The network contains 60 lines. Hence the average line length is 21.6 miles. The average journey length may be half that or 10 miles (compared with 25 miles for the national network as a whole). On that basis the Community Rail network may carry 236 million passenger-miles annually. Dividing by the network length and by the days in the year yields an average daily two-way flow of 500 people, or 250 in each direction.

If these 250 people transferred to coaches, each carrying 20 people, 13 vehicles per day, or one half-full coach every hour, would suffice – illustrating the trivial use to which these invaluable rights of way are put. Many of them offer perhaps a one- or two-car 'train' every couple of hours.

Taxpayers' subsidy

Community Rail's annual subsidy is £300 million. That corresponds to £5 million per year per line or to £230,000 per year per route-mile or to 127 pence per passenger-mile. Add the fares and we can see at a glance that the cost is substantially above that of an ordinary car, let alone travel by coach. Probably an on-demand minibus would do the job at a fraction of the cost of the trains.

Likely effect on local economies

National railways carry 2 per cent of motorised passenger-journeys or 5.5 per cent of passenger-miles, concentrated in the South-East.

Hence, in areas served by the Community Rail network it would be surprising if more than 0.5 per cent of journeys or 1.5 per cent of passenger-miles were by rail. With numbers as low as those, how can any person, let alone members of the Institute of Chartered Accountants, conclude that the Community Rail network is important to the local economy? Probably its contribution is so small as to be impossible to measure, and very much less than the £300 million per year (£230,000 per route-mile) contributed by the taxpayer.

Infrastructure costs

Infrastructure costs for the scarcely used Community Rail network are cited as £100,000 per track-mile. In contrast the capital and current account expenditures on the motorway and trunk road network amounted to £1,038 million and £982 million respectively in 2003/04, providing a total of £2,020 million (Department for Transport 2004; table 1.15). A mid-range estimate of the lane length is 44,000 km or 28,000 miles (Appendix to Transport-Watch facts sheet 1, 2005). Hence the expenditure per lane mile was circa £72,000, over half of which was capital. Probably the £72,000 should be halved for comparison with the rural rail network, since that network will have enjoyed little capital expenditure. That provides £36,000 per lane mile – less than half the £100,000 required per track-mile for the scarcely used Community Rail Network.

Rolling-stock costs

The cost per carriage for Community Rail is set by the SRA at £100,000 per year for leasing and heavy maintenance, amounting to between 50 and 75 per cent of vehicle costs. Hence full annual vehicle costs have the range £133,000 to £200,000. If there are 75 seats the cost per seat per year has the range £1,800 to £27,700. In comparison a brand-new 50-seat motor coach may cost £150,000. If that were to be repaid over as little as ten years at the Treasury Discount rate of 3.5 per cent, and if maintenance costs amount to 7.5 per cent of capital, then the annual cost would be £30,000, providing a cost per seat of £600 per year – three to 4.5 times less than for the railway carriage.

Widths – potential as roads[1]

The track width for a train is 4 feet 8.5 inches. It is derived from the carts being dragged by pit ponies 150 years ago. Bridge abutments, tunnels and viaducts on double-track railways, however, offer a clear width seldom less than 7.3 metres (24 feet) – the same as the carriageway width required for a two-way trunk road. Elsewhere double-track railways offer a level width of 8.5 metres (28 feet) on tangents and more on bends. Single-track railways offer 13 feet between bridge abutments but many were built on double-track formations. Hence the widths of most railways would accommodate carriageways the same width as that for new (single-carriageway) trunk roads, but not the 3-metre verges that form part of the design standard for green-field construction. Effective verges are, however, generally absent on most ordinary roads and would serve little or no purpose on railway alignments.

The European carriageway width for a two-way road is 7 metres, and at one time the standard for Scottish trunk roads was 5.5 metres

---

1   The source for the railway widths cited here is British Railways.

(18 feet). It may also be noted that there are many 'A' roads 6 metres wide on which lorries and coaches operate without difficulty.

As for headroom, clearances above rail top are normally 4.16 metres (13 feet 8 inches), increased to 4.77 metres (15 feet 8 inches) where there is overhead electrification. Road level would be 300 millimetres (1 foot) below rail top. Hence, without altering tunnels and bridges, the clearances available are from 4.46 metres up to 5.07 metres. In many parts of the world the required headroom is 4.5 metres.

Although car transporters in the UK are often 4.9 metres high, nearly all container lorries are less than 4.3 metres high. Further, the standard height for international transport is 4 metres. Double-deck buses range in height from 3.9 metres to 4.44 metres. A headroom clearance above the vehicles of 200 millimetres is adequate.

Against that background the notion that railways are too narrow or lack adequate headroom should be dismissed.

The inquiry into rural rail

At the inquiry into rural rail none of that was considered. Instead, the committee's inaugural press notice set the terms of reference as examining:

- 'the importance of rural railways to the communities they serve';
- 'the prospects for innovative approaches to funding and management of such railways';
- 'the prospects of traffic growth on such railways';
- 'the impact of measures such as bus substitution for rail services'.

The committee has yet to report but the hearings were not

encouraging – among other factors it inquired into 'through ticketing' and the 'integration of local bus and rail services'. We comment: (a) through ticketing is likely to benefit perhaps one in one hundred rail journeys; and (b) since perhaps half of 1 per cent of the population in a rural area uses rail at all regularly, most of them being car drivers, the demand for a bus service to the stations will be vanishingly small. Even in a town like Northampton (population 200,000) bus services to the railway station are periodically demanded, only to founder for lack of ongoing demand.

Meanwhile the chair of the committee, Gwyneth Dunwoody, was in the cabinet that made the decision to keep open 150 miles of the Central Wales Line. That was an entirely political decision, as illustrated by Lord Marsh, who, in the House of Lords on 2 March 1982, related that, when Minister of Transport, he had put forward to cabinet an unanswerable case for closure. He explained that it would be cheaper to provide each passenger with a chauffeur-driven Bentley than to keep the line open. The Welsh secretary then piped up, 'But, Minister, this line runs through six marginal constituencies.' Needless to say, the line is still open.

Separately from the committee's proceedings the government is clearly exercised by the extraordinary cost of rail. Hence Alistair Darling, the Secretary of State for Transport, was widely reported as saying with regard to rural rail that the government is not in the business of carting fresh air around the countryside. We comment: it is not the fresh air which is the major problem. Instead it is the waste of the rights of way.

Conclusion

The government and local communities need to decide whether the invaluable rights of way making up the rural rail network should be (a) converted to motor roads so that they that may act as feeders to the main lines; or (b) abandoned to rabbits and hedgehogs; or (c) preserved as full-sized, fully working transport museums.

Unfortunately for the nation, and more particularly for the taxpayer and road user, the likelihood is that subsidy will continue to keep rural railways open for some time, while in the longer term many rural lines will close and be abandoned as in the past.

The reason for this awful prospect is that politicians appear to have no grasp of numbers and a keen eye for the voter, however misled. Perhaps a low-tax economy would lead to less folly and perhaps the government, instead of dealing with detail, should address strategic issues; for example, it should ensure that the rail network, and rural rail in particular, continues in transport use instead of being closed down piecemeal over the next 100 years.

A radical alternative to government direction would be to remove subsidy entirely from transport, leaving the market to determine the proportion of the nation's wealth that should be spent in that sector. It is beyond the scope of this paper to examine the consequences of this, but the prospect is exciting. A starting point may be to look at the profit to the exchequer from road and rail and to compare that with the profit to be made from that land if in other use. Here we note that currently each lane-mile of the motorway and trunk road network pays the exchequer £(275–360) thousand per year in taxes (net of expenditure) compared with a loss per track-mile on the national rail network of £(225–325) thousand per year (Transport-Watch, 2005b). Converted rural rail may not match the motorway and trunk roads for profit, but the rural rail network does compete quite well with the national network for losses (£230,000 per *route*-mile; see above).

In any event, taking transport out of the political arena into the free market would avoid the astonishing waste of resources that rail, particularly rural rail, has led to over these last 50 years.

References

British Railways Board (1963), *The Reshaping of Britain's Railways*, London: HMSO.

Dalgleish, A. (1982), *The Truth about Transport*, London: Centre for Policy Studies (2nd edition, 1993).

Department for Transport (DfT) (2004), *Transport Statistics Great Britain* (2004 edition), London: TSO (The Stationery Office).

House of Commons Transport Select Committee (2004), *The Future of the Railway*, London: Stationery Office.

Strategic Rail Authority (2004a), *Community Rail Development: A consultation paper on a strategy for Community Railways*, London: Strategic Rail Authority.

Strategic Rail Authority (2004b), *Community Rail Development Strategy*, London: Strategic Rail Authority.

Transport-Watch (2004), *Facts Sheet 5: Fuel Consumptions*, Northampton: Transport-Watch, available from www.transwatch.co.uk.

Transport-Watch (2005a), *Facts Sheet 1: Capacity, average flow and density of use*, Northampton: Transport-Watch, available from www.transwatch.co.uk.

Transport-Watch (2005b), *Facts Sheet 4: Subsidy to rail and profits from roads*, Northampton: Transport-Watch, available from www.transwatch.co.uk.

Withrington, P. (2004) 'Reigniting the railway conversion debate', *Economic Affairs*, 24(2): 56–9.

PART III

FARMING, FORESTRY AND THE ENVIRONMENT

8 HOW MAFF CAUSED THE 2001 FOOT-AND-MOUTH EPIDEMIC

David Campbell and Bob Lee

[T]here is a real danger that extensive governmental intervention in the economic system may lead to the protection of those responsible for harmful effects being carried too far.

RONALD COASE (1960: 28)

Though the most important of the three inquiries the government commissioned into the 2001 epidemic of foot-and-mouth disease (FMD) was the Lessons Learned inquiry chaired by Dr Iain Anderson, the nature of the steps the government has taken since the epidemic to reform its disease control policy shows that the main lesson of this appalling episode has not been learned at all. The epidemic was not merely badly managed by the then Ministry of Agriculture, Fisheries and Food (MAFF), as is now universally acknowledged, but was *caused* by its livestock policies. As the new Department for Environment, Food and Rural Affairs (Defra) still fails to recognise this, the reformed disease control policy will almost certainly cause another epidemic in the future.

Foot-and-mouth disease

The nature of FMD and what it means for control of the disease are still generally misunderstood by the public. It is not generally known that FMD has no implications for the human food chain, and its impact on animal welfare is typically seriously overestimated. FMD is indeed an extremely contagious disease, the most infectious disease of livestock known. But one of the reasons it is so infectious is that it occasions only a very low rate of mortality. For most adult animals, FMD is comparable to flu in humans, though sometimes accompanied by painful sores, and the major problem for disease control is that animals with FMD, displaying only symptoms so mild as not to be detectable by normal husbandry, live to transmit the disease. The FMD virus can survive for weeks or months in infected animals and their wastes, and it is able to be transmitted by direct contact with carrier animals and by contact with their discharges, including their exhalations.

As it is so contagious, FMD, which has been known to livestock rearers for at least 400 years, remains endemic in a sporadic fashion in most livestock rearing areas of the world. Its suppression requires resources available only to the agricultural sectors of wealthy countries. It was sporadically endemic throughout western Europe until 1990, being then suppressed by huge European Union (EU) investment in prophylactic vaccination, supported, when such vaccinations failed, by the 'stamping out' of outbreaks by slaughter of infected animals and animals at risk of infection. The United Kingdom is one of a very few countries where vaccination has never been used. In 1990, the EU completely abandoned prophylactic vaccination, and this, together with the phasing out of veterinary frontier controls under the single market, has created an enormous fully susceptible livestock population. Until the 2001 epidemic, however, the EU had managed to stamp out outbreaks quickly.

The Animal Health Act 1981 gave MAFF the powers to implement stamping out in the UK. Stamping out is possible only as a government policy, for it envisages the quick slaughter of infected and at-risk animals in a way that no private body without the powers of the state could possibly undertake. Stamping out really is a policy aimed at nipping outbreaks in the bud. For it to work, FMD has to be detected, assessed and limited quickly, and infected and at-risk animals have to be slaughtered and disposed of quickly.

The 2001 outbreak

In 2001, absolutely none of this happened. MAFF's initial response to the outbreak of the disease was hopelessly inadequate. It had no reliable monitoring in place and was far too slow to identify the danger. By the time it did so, infected animals had been moved around the country, spreading the disease to what proved to be an unknown and uncontrollable extent. MAFF was even then very slow to take effective action to deal with what had happened by working out the epidemiology of the outbreak or imposing biosecurity measures to limit it. On the government's own account, a single outbreak on a farm in Northumbria was able to lead to a situation in which almost the entire country was infected, with the disease having been seeded to an uncontrollable extent before the first case was even detected. It is impossible in a short compass adequately to convey the incompetence of MAFF's disease control policy (for a more full account, see Campbell and Lee, 2003a). In the end, stamping out was, in a most important sense, abandoned, because, as the extent of the disease was more or less unknown, the slaughter became general in an attempt to carry out preventive, 'firewall' culling under the 'contiguous cull' policy.

Under the contiguous cull, animals on premises sharing a

boundary with premises suspected of being infected, or in some areas on premises within 3 kilometres of suspected infected premises, were killed on the flimsiest, or in truth no real, suspicion of infection, and the army had to be drafted in to make sure the consequent immense slaughter – the largest in history – could be carried out. In the end, almost 11 million animals were killed. Perhaps 90 per cent of these were uninfected. The disease was stamped out in a sense, but only because the contiguous cull had become a policy of killing more or less any animal in disregard of epidemiological evidence or the economic, human and animal welfare costs. In particular, it was impossible to ensure that all these animals were killed humanely. Hundreds of thousands or even millions of animals will not have been killed in the ways required by animal welfare legislation, and great numbers will have been killed in ways so horribly cruel that they should occasion lasting national shame.

In the light of this catastrophe and the appalling performance of MAFF, the government has sought to prepare better contingency plans for the future. With hindsight of the epidemic, all sorts of extra provisions for dealing with another outbreak have been proposed. Greater legal powers of slaughter,[1] greater numbers of veterinarians to identify the disease, greater numbers of officials to monitor biosecurity measures, greater numbers of rendering plants to dispose of slaughtered animals, greater amounts of emergency vaccine to treat animals suspected of being infected,

---

1   MAFF's slaughter powers under the Animal Health Act 1981, envisaging the implementation of stamping out, did not authorise preventive slaughter under the contiguous cull, which therefore was a massive *ultra vires* exercise of government powers. The 1981 act has been amended in an attempt to make preventive culling lawful in future by authorising the slaughter of 'any animal' (Campbell and Lee, 2003b).

and so on, are being considered. The revised disease control plan has recently been trialled, and while this must be a sort of improvement as no such trialling had taken place prior to 2001, the trial has merely made obvious what was in any case perfectly clear.[2] The expenditure needed for Defra to ensure that any future outbreak will be satisfactorily controlled is absolutely enormous; indeed, it would require a perfectly fanciful sum to do this. As has been realised in non-agricultural sectors, throwing money at the problem in this way is terribly mistaken. The correct answer to the question of how much public money should be spent on disease control is not, as is generally being claimed, a lot more; the correct answer is a lot less.

Livestock rearing practices, risk and incentives

For the risk of an epidemic is not merely a question of the amount of investment in cure. It is also, and more importantly, a question of the livestock rearing practices that produce the risk. The issues would normally be obvious in business outside of farming. Imagine a businessperson who wants to set up a factory that uses combustible materials. There is naturally a risk that a fire will occur and harm the factory, the employees and the surrounding area, and the factory owner is normally legally liable for this harm. This risk can never be completely eliminated, though it can, of course, be increased or diminished depending on the behaviour of the factory owner and his employees.

---

2   The trial simulated eleven outbreaks. But in 2001 there were certainly at least 50, and there may well have been over 100, outbreaks before the first case was identified. The trial has made no attempt to deal with this, though it is the crucial issue; indeed, it could not deal with it.

To deal with the ineliminable risk, the factory owner must take out insurance. The cost of the insurance will depend on how likely the fire is and how much damage it would cause. To keep his insurance as low as possible, the factory owner will be careful and will take steps to make his employees careful. He will site his factory in an area where the damage a fire will cause will be kept low, perhaps in a remote area. However, there may be good reasons to take a larger risk, because, say, use of a particularly combustible material yields great efficiencies in the manufacturing process, or being near to population concentrations saves transport costs. The factory owner will be inclined to take these risks, but his potential liability and insurance premium will go up accordingly. In the normal way, the profits of risk-taking will be balanced against the costs of liability and insurance, and the optimum level of risk will be run because of the discipline imposed by the costs of insurance.

If one substitutes 'livestock rearer' or 'dealer' for 'factory owner' in this example, one can see how MAFF caused the 2001 epidemic. By taking over responsibilities for disease control, and normally giving very generous compensation for slaughtered stock, MAFF has made the costs of disease control irrelevant to the livestock industry.[3] The risk that is an 'internal' cost in the factory example is made an 'externality' because disease control is provided as a 'public good', and the economic incentive of the livestock industry to pay any attention to that risk is much reduced. During the epidemic, the manifest selfishness, particularly of the

---

3   The consequences of the epidemic were very different for different persons in the livestock industry, ranging from tragedy and hardship for some to enormous enrichment for others, and we are anxious that our general statements here should not be taken as denying the plight of those in the former category.

national leadership of the National Farmers' Union (NFU), exasperated the government and disgusted the general public. This conduct *was* sometimes disgusting, but MAFF's policies encouraged the livestock industry to take this line. MAFF created a situation of 'moral hazard' in which the livestock industry devised its livestock rearing practices in disregard of the costs of disease control because those costs are an externality to them.

In particular, although the most obvious fact about FMD is that it is so contagious that to move animals is enormously risky, there are tens of millions of live animal movements across the UK and the EU every year. This was the underlying cause of the 2001 epidemic. Infected animals were shipped the length of the country and so brought into contact with animals from most other parts of the country, which were then themselves moved on. A policy that was intended to spread the disease would not be much different. These livestock movements are supposed to be safe because of the biosecurity procedures, but not only does the livestock industry have a poor record of compliance with these procedures, the practices themselves cannot possibly be so completely effective as to prevent future outbreaks, and the volume of livestock movement will always threaten to turn an outbreak into an epidemic.

The main lesson of modern regulatory theory is that economic regulation based on the use of criminal sanctions is likely to be seriously deficient and economic incentives are a superior regulatory mechanism. Effective inspection and criminal prosecution of the entire livestock industry is impossibly costly, and is a draconian measure that would not be needed if the industry was liable for the costs of insurance against the disease. The owners of the particular farm claimed to be the source of the 2001 epidemic have been prosecuted for their (unarguably disgusting and blameworthy) rearing practices. But it was the blameless movement of sheep by a neighbouring farmer which was the main cause of the seeding of the epidemic, and this prosecution is merely fruitless scapegoating.

The stamping-out policy is an example of 'blackboard economics'. *If* FMD can be quickly detected, *if* it can be quickly localised, *if* infected and at-risk animals can be identified, slaughtered and disposed of quickly, and *if* other appropriate biosecurity measures can be quickly put in place, it will work. But while stamping out may work to stop localised outbreaks, there is absolutely no reason to believe that it can ever work on a large scale, and it will eventually be needed on a large scale because of rearing practices that always threaten to turn an outbreak into an epidemic. The only reason stamping out was ever thought to be a sensible response to a large-scale outbreak is that it was never properly costed for that purpose.

Now that the call for better contingency planning is leading to the exclusive use of stamping out being properly costed, it will in all likelihood be abandoned.[4] Widespread use of vaccination may improve the handling of the disease and in particular reduce the amount of appalling cruelty. But it is very costly itself and cannot possibly solve all the problems or eliminate all the cruelty. If vaccination is not adopted and the livestock rearing practices that create an epidemic are not changed, stamping out is again bound

---

4   Certain influential livestock interests use the status of being FMD free without vaccination to obtain an important international trade advantage, and their anxiety to protect that status stalled MAFF's use of emergency vaccination in 2001, and appears to be having the same effect on Defra. A firmer grip of the situation is being taken by the EU, however, which was guilty of many sins of omission prior to the 2001 epidemic, and the direction of EU policy would appear to be towards mandating vaccination as a response to a serious outbreak.

to decay into killing everything when the next major outbreak occurs. But even if vaccination is adopted, if those practices are not changed, we are still headed for another catastrophe.

If the government told the factory owner in our example that, if his factory burns down, he will not be liable to anyone else and will be compensated many times the value of his own losses, we should not be surprised when the factory burns down. The factory owner might even deliberately burn it down, but this is less important than the fact that he will not take the same care and will take on more risks than he would if the fire would cause him a loss. Some livestock rearers may have infected their own stock during the epidemic, but this has not been proven and it is far less important than the fact that the livestock industry's normal practices caused that epidemic, and that it adopted those practices because MAFF's policies led to them disregarding FMD as an externality. Had FMD been treated as a normal business risk to be borne by those engaged in the business, it could have been relatively easily handled as a normal business expense. The livestock rearing practices that caused the epidemic would never have been adopted.

Conclusion

Change far more radical than the government shows any capacity to undertake must take place. Unless the livestock industry is made to internalise the costs of disease, including FMD control, and devise its livestock rearing practices so that it will not be so very reckless about spreading the disease, then there is every likelihood that there will be another epidemic. We believe it is inevitable unless FMD control is no longer treated as a public good but rather as an ordinary business expense. What the government now proposes is aimed at keeping the same livestock rearing (and meat marketing) practices going, and tinkering with the public disease control measures that catastrophically failed in 2001 and will always be susceptible to such failure. It will be as effective a response to disease control as MAFF changing its name to Defra, the characteristic public relations response of this government to the dreadful catastrophe its policies have *caused*.

References

Campbell, D. and R. Lee (2003a), '"Carnage by computer": the blackboard economics of the 2001 foot and mouth epidemic', *Social and Legal Studies*, 12: 425–59.

Campbell, D. and R. Lee (2003b), 'The power to panic: the Animal Health Act 2002', *Public Law*, autumn, pp. 382–96.

Coase, R. (1960), 'The problem of social cost', *Journal of Law and Economics*, 3: 1–44.

9 FARMING AND THE TAXPAYER: PAYING FOR FOOD AND COUNTRYSIDE IN THE NEW AGE OF FREE TRADE

Richard D. North

Farming has been at the centre of British politics for 200 years. Even as industrialisation transformed the economy in the nineteenth century, free trade in food caused many of the fissures around which parties formed. In 2003, reforms to EU agriculture policy were perhaps rightly described as being 'as important as any since the repeal of the corn laws' in 1846.[1] The questions have always been deceptively simple. Since we can grow food, shouldn't we aim for self-sufficiency and food security? Or: why would a wet, grey country try to buck the market and deny itself foreign food? The 1846 answer held for a century. In the islands that gave the world Adam Smith but had to import French chefs, we were and are bound to discuss food not merely as a matter of nutrition, taste or fashion but also as a matter of comparative advantage.

In the nineteenth century the English decided to eat food sourced for the convenience of factory workers and their employers, not of the farm labourer, or the yeoman farmer and his landlord. But that policy didn't kill off a British agriculture dominated by progressives. Even when the North Americans and – much later – the French, Danes and New Zealanders caught up, industrialised British farmers could survive against their competi-

---

1   George Dunn, of the UK Tenant Farmers' Association, giving evidence to the House of Commons Select Committee on Environment, Food and Rural Affairs, January 2004.

tors' cheaper land and better weather. These were the years when an urbanised country fell in love with its countryside, and farmers were thought of as natural, unconscious guardians of its loveliness.

In the twentieth century, Hitler made self-sufficiency as necessary as Napoleon once had. For 50 years we have been happy to shelter our farmers behind trade barriers and to throw money at them. Discussion of the CAP (Common Agriculture Policy) was subsumed and almost lost in the vast, fractured debate on the EU in general. Yet the £30 billion the EU spends on its farmers constitutes half the EU budget. While many services (health, education, broadcasting) remain statist, farming is the last state-run production industry. The situation was probably tolerated for so long because consumers didn't associate the £3 billion support given to UK farmers with their own shopping basket. They vaguely understood that at least some of the money came from Germany.

Over the course of the last half-century, a vociferous minority of the public learned a new aesthetic: they yearned for a premodern countryside. Worse, they knew that CAP-fuelled farmers had had a big hand in robbing them of it. Even so, campaigning against the CAP was half-hearted because the various ideologues who hated it hated each other more. That is to say, the free trade, free market right that disliked the CAP's corporatism has never wanted or been able to make common cause with the leftish conservationists and environmentalists who disliked the deepening factorification of the farmscape that it helped fund. Besides, as the animal welfarists pointed out, the market – and not the EU – was causing a good deal of industrialisation of animal farming all by itself. The market might have made some farmers more destructive than even the CAP did.

In the end, the underlying engine of reform was the liberalisation of world trade, which has even been embraced (in part and grudgingly) by Oxfam and other cheerleaders of Third World development. And it has been helped by the widening of the EU to include tens of thousands of new farmers whom it would be impossible, even if it were desirable or desired, to support.

Producing butterflies

However it was that they clung to the public purse, farmers have seemed like John Bull with a begging-bowl. Like all victims of welfare, they became unattractive: addicted but resentful. To their credit, the farmers' leaders – even the National Farmers' Union and the Country Landowners' Association – have long understood and embraced the case for reform. It is very likely that – absent its being trapped in the EU – Britain would have followed New Zealand in abandoning subsidies years ago. It is possible that, absent the EU, the American farmers would have been half-weaned off support as well. Following World Trade Organisation and EU decisions made in the past year, farmers and politicians are working out how to shift an unchanged quantum of support from production to social and environmental subsidy. That will reduce the trade-distorting effects of the CAP, and largely silence the claims of Oxfam, Bono and Bob Geldof that the EU causes starvation in Africa.

But the free trade logic will grind on, and farmers seem to believe that subsidies of every kind will be reduced dramatically within a decade or so. They freely discuss the interim arrangements as a relatively gentle 'detox' alternative to the more brutal 'cold turkey' that the free market people might prefer they suffer, but they tell politicians that they accept that the drug of subsidy simply won't be there soon.[2]

Peculiarly, we are likely to go from a system under which farmers were well paid to do pretty much what they liked to one in which they have to deliver all sorts of 'extras' while getting low prices. Their impacts on the landscape, soil and watercourses, their treatment of animals and their use of fuel will all be scruti-nised and regulated (or 'voluntarily' policed) much more. British farmers will be required to maintain regimes that are far more costly than those imposed in other parts of the world. They will struggle to persuade consumers that their product is worth the extra: it is work they are bad at. It will be especially difficult for as long as supermarkets believe that most of their customers care mostly about cheapness.

Let's put this brutally. Many of the British have been happy to eat rubbish, and have done so while the supermarkets (let alone foreign holidays) have offered them interesting alternatives. Alongside a commoditised market in junk, there has grown up a niche organic market whose rationale has been to pose a radical alternative to the mainstream. These two strands are for the time being at war. The organic sector will lose market share as soon as conventional farming slightly greens itself. And the conventional, pesticide-based mainstream has much more to learn from the pseudo-peasants of the organic tendency. The latter cooperate so as to match the power of the supermarket buyer. They have under-stood how to pin a narrative to their produce. They talk – and mostly believe – nonsense and sell at high prices often surprisingly unhealthy or dreary food to anxiety-ridden consumers who also

2   The House of Commons Select Committee on Environment, Food and Farming's Seventh Report, April 2004, is a rich source on the contemporary debate.

talk and believe nonsense.[3] But they are one of the best examples of the market at work.

Let's not subsidise organic

Politicians have been in a muddle about organic food and farming. Caught up in a mantra of 'sustainable development', and wary of organic's vociferous middle-class fan club, they have sought to endorse it, have given it a few tens of millions of subsidy, but not dared celebrate it wholeheartedly. How to praise it without condemning the mainstream?

They may also realise that from a public policy point of view, organic farms are of very limited use. There is good evidence that organic farming is not, of itself, much better for the birds and the bees (let alone for consumers) than stuff sprayed with chemicals (Tinker, 2000). The environmental NGOs have spread nonsense for years and the newer boutique farmers have loved them for it. It is true that some early pesticides poisoned some predator birds and some river creatures (otters, for instance). Those chemicals were almost all banned years ago and aren't the issue now. But there were other factors at work, and some of the most important remain. Chemicals have allowed farmers to wage war on pests, and unfortunately that includes the weeds (that is, the wild flowers) and insects that birds and landscape painters and photographers live on. They have sown crops in the autumn, when the fallow ground used to be good for birds. But organic farmers are good for wildlife only because they promote it; 'conventional' farmers aren't, because – at the moment – they spray it.

---

3   Judith Woods, 'Is organic food really worth the money', *Daily Telegraph*, 27 October 2004.

The unsung equation is this. The vast majority of English land is in the hands of mainstream farming. Any given percentage of environmental improvement – even if small – we get from that land is worth far more than whatever we have got or can ever get from the tiny percentage of land that is or will ever be 'organic' (a few per cent now, and most of it grassland) (Defra/National Statistics, 2005).

The conventional farmer can grow huge amounts of cheap food, and has the potential to do so alongside a vibrant wildlife. That's what chemicals and crop regimes already deliver wherever anyone bothers to 'tickle' the system in favour of nature. It's also what farmers are moving towards as they negotiate changes to the subsidy system. They are busy demonstrating how green they can be, granted that their remaining subsidies depend on this new pitch. In the bureaucratic argot: as their subsidy is 'decoupled' from production, one of the 'modulations' by which they can hang on to it is 'cross-compliance' with a rising tide of the slightly greener things they should have done decades ago if they had understood where their market was going. They will now need to learn how to sell the merits of their 'conventional' farming: to say that, refocused, chemicals and sheds are good for food, landscape and animals.

There will be far fewer farmers in the future. It was a bad year but only a historic trend which saw 17,000 people leave farming in the twelve months to June 2003.[4] That trend is as old as civilisation, and has been slowed only slightly by subsidies. No amount of money will produce replacements for the present generation of hill farmers, for instance. Modern culture does not produce the

---

4   *Farm: The Independent Voice of Farmers*, 12 February 2004, available online at: www.farm.org.uk/FM_Content.aspx?action=detail&id=169.

near-peasants who have traditionally run our most attractive, bleak landscapes. There and elsewhere, there may be an influx of pseudo-peasants. But even organic, free-range farming is likely to succumb to the advantages of scale, and fall into the hands of a proficient and adventurous few. There may well be two tracks for farmers, irrespective of their preference for the conventional or the niche model of farming: some will throw lots of capital at their land, and others won't. Equally canny operators will choose either high- or low-input approaches to solvency in a business that will presumably remain prey to roller-coaster income fluctuations and vicious cycles of under- and over-production.

It is just possible that the taxpayer will be prepared to continue to subsidise farmers to produce butterflies. But, as Sir Richard Packer (2001), one-time permanent secretary at the erstwhile Ministry of Agriculture, Fisheries and Food (now Defra), said in a Centre for Policy Studies pamphlet, we shouldn't believe that the answer is to keep subsidising lots of farmers, but to pay for environmental gains rather than production. We've got to get it out of our heads that we are in the business of populating the landscape with hicks at all.

Modern taxpayers may pay for environmental outcomes, but they aren't likely to fall for looking after producers, especially tweedy types in four-by-fours who are believed to have killed off the farm birds while gruffly seeing off ramblers. What is much less clear is what level of wildlife friendliness should be 'normal' for farmers. What is the number of butterflies or space for pigs which society can reasonably expect farmers to produce without special reward? Set the amounts too high and one is pricing farmers out of any chance of international competition, and in any case flirting with a new form of Stalinisation. Set them too low and we leave too many of the 'externalities' of farming to be picked up by non-farmers.

Whatever the compulsory level, the trick to getting even more animal welfare, more birds and bees, more hedges, copses and ponds, is for conservationists, supermarkets and even the taxpayer to pay for them, but to pay only for the welfare, wildlife or habitat. When farmers see these extras as crops, we'll get huge amounts of them, because actually they're quite easy to deliver. The mechanisms have been outlined by many people, and perhaps especially by the Royal Agricultural Society of England.

In one version, a supermarket, or a conservation group, even the taxpayer if all else fails, would advertise that there is a pot of money with which to fund contracts for the production of this or that bird (or insect, or whatever) which is in decline. Farmers, singly or in cooperation with one another, make sealed bids in the manner of an auction. If they deliver the birds (or snakes, or whatever) they get the money. It doesn't matter whether they use chemicals or hate them. It's the outcome which matters, not the method of production, or the numbers of producers.

Connecting customers with food production will also be important. If consumers started to care about the provenance of their food, they might buy some of the externalities they are supposed to like but don't presently connect with shopping. Supermarkets have been brilliant at delivering cheap food smothered in pictures of a long-dead countryside of straw-sucking peasants in smocks. Farmers and retailers shouldn't be expected to be social workers, propagandists or even conservationists. But they should, as professionals, be uncomfortable with the way their customers are buying food, which does so little for the countryside in which it is produced. Supermarkets could be enhancing their bottom line, and making us even more proud of them, by competing to identify their products with the wider scene. Some already seem to be serious about this approach. The trick will be to abandon the purist excesses of the organic myth and instead to discuss and offer a sort of golden mean. Within a decade the food business could prove that 'Grown in Britain' means something valuable. If it doesn't, farmers will be condemned to pay for an improved world out of their own pockets and supermarkets will be accused of starving their suppliers of the means to be useful.

There may be lots of good news in the pipeline. Less subsidy for production may reduce the opportunity cost of waging a less intense war on wildlife, and land cheap enough to encourage it. We may decide that large areas of land near the sea should return to salt marsh. The hills may return to scrubby woodland and bog. Free-ranging animals on cheap, soggy and steep land may well be the best use for it. At the other end of the scale, intensive agriculture will get better at being useful. Farmers keeping animals in sheds may well have the tricks and technologies – and breeding stock – which make them even more profitable as well as welfare conscious. Shed farming allows the greater part of a farmer's income to come from a tiny covered acreage while the greater part of his land is used to turn chicken, cow or pig manure into a gorgeous habitat for wildlife and people.

We will probably urbanise much more land. Planners ought to be far more imaginative – and politicians far bolder – in envisioning the countryside they want to get other people to fund. We could easily be producing large quantities of houses set in great wooded landscapes, with kestrels hunting over the roads that lead to them. There is very little wrong with our slightly crowded island landscape that cannot be put right with the judicious use of a JCB. Rising transport costs, or road congestion, might complicate this picture – but we have no idea whether 'hyper-mobility', or global warming, will really worry our children and grandchildren, and whether even rurban dwellers need be hooked on either.

Ponds, wetlands, hillocks, meadows, woods – we can create them all, and some will be farms and others will be housing estates and technology parks. Some of them will be managed by the children of our present generation of farmers. Many more, probably, will be created by dynamic incomers who also love the countryside. And none of these rural entrepreneurs and professionals will be allowed to fantasise that they've a God-given right to get a living from it.

How much farming policy do we need?

Obviously, my preference is for as little policy as possible: that's the free market dream. There is hardly any desirable countryside policy that is not widely popular. Handsome landscape, well-cared-for animals and a rich wildlife are all much admired. They are also highly marketable and quite cheap to achieve. They need not be the victim of market failure. But that is no guarantee that they will happen. Unless government has the courage to say that it really does not want to get involved, the farmers, supermarkets and public will settle for the rather shabby default we have known so far. That is: the state's imposition of low standards, which it reluctantly enforces. We can hope for better than that. But, as in the dismantling of any state machinery, it will require other – voluntary – players to see and seek advantage in doing things, and doing them better, for themselves.

There is some sign that these sorts of view are becoming orthodox among farmers. ADAS, the hived-off erstwhile Ministry of Agriculture advisory service, has been celebrating its 35 years of life with a 'blue skies' project whose conclusions are surely fairly mainstream and would not shock a free market person.[5] ADAS supposes that farmers may have many pressures on them in the future (some of them regulatory), but assumes more surely that they will not be able to expect very much state support or even guidance in facing them.

References

Defra/National Statistics (2005), *Organic Statistics*, London: Defra/National Statistics.

Packer, R. (2001), *A Policy for Agriculture: Ending state interference*, London: Centre for Policy Studies.

Tinker, P. B. (ed.) (2000), *Shades of Green: A review of UK farming systems*, London: Royal Agricultural Society of England.

---

5   www.adas.co.uk/bluesky35/.

10 THE FARMING LOBBY: A WANING POWER?

Séan Rickard

The issue under consideration in this paper is the extent to which the UK farm lobby has lost, or is losing, the power to ensure that farmers and farming remain highly protected and subsidised. The farming lobby is defined as those organisations that can legimately claim to represent the economic interests of farmers. The farm lobby is a sub-set of the agricultural lobby and *primus inter pares* is the National Farmers' Union (NFU) of England and Wales. The position of the NFU, together with its sister organisations in Scotland and Northern Ireland, as the 'voice of British farming' was cemented by the 1947 Agricultural Act, which essentially set in law the involvement of the NFU in all aspects of government agricultural policy-making (Grant, 1983). By making the NFU a statutory consultee in agricultural policy the government handed the union unprecedented 'insider' status with the power to influence the level and incidence of agricultural support.

The UK's accession to membership of the European Community (EC) in 1973 transferred many of the decisions regarding farm support to the Agricultural Council, where the UK had to negotiate for its objectives. In the early years membership of the EC did not significantly change the power of the three NFUs to influence government thinking on agriculture. The three NFUs were still formally consulted in an annual review of the industry and both sides had a vested interest in the pursuit of increased agricultural output. In retrospect the 1970s can be viewed as the years of 'high farming' for British farmers: by the end of the 1980s a combination of growing surpluses, broader political support for rural and environmental issues and a greater emphasis on market liberalisation all served to place the farm lobby in a defensive position.

This paper argues that the NFU of England and Wales remains *primus inter pares* within a weakened farm lobby. Its 'insider' status is now less formal and it has been forced to adjust its policy stance in line with a changing external and political environment. The structure of this paper is as follows. The next section shows that despite an apparent decline in the power of the three NFUs and the Country Landowners' Association (CLA) to influence policy, the returns to land owners have performed extremely well. The second section analyses the external forces that now condition and constrain government agricultural policy. The final section considers the challenge to the farm lobby from more militant and more broadly based countryside organisations.

Objectives and members

The stated objectives for agricultural policy in the UK, by both politicians and the farm lobby, are varied, but over the period since the UK's accession to what is now the European Union (EU) they have included, in broad chronological order, self-sufficiency, the balance of trade, secure supplies at low prices, rural employment, farm incomes and the protection of the countryside. The objectives have been very much in line with other developed nations (Winter, 1989), and in attempting to achieve these objectives there has been a massive transfer of income to farmers amounting, according to one estimate, to the equivalent of at least

£5 billion per year since 1973 at current prices (Rickard, 2004). But of the objectives set out above, only the provision of secure supplies of agricultural produce at low prices could be said to have been fully achieved.

Farm incomes rose markedly with UK membership of the EC, but since 1973, as revealed in the government's annual review of the UK farming industry, total income from farming (on a per capita basis) has displayed a declining trend of a little over 1 per cent per year: see Figure 2 (Defra, 2005). The farming population – farmers and farm workers – has declined at a similar rate, though the decline masks a dramatic decline in the number of employees and a substantial shift to part-time or seasonal working by both farmers and employees. As for the balance of trade, after some years of apparent improvement – apparent because the gain was not set against the cost of export subsidies – the net balance has remained fairly constant over the past decade at a little over 1 per cent of GDP (ibid.). From this perspective the activities of the farm lobby would appear to have been less than fully effective. But viewed from the perspective of land values, one might very reasonably draw a very different conclusion. Between 1971 and 1972 agricultural land values increased by more than 100 per cent and have continued to rise at an underlying rate of 5 per cent per year since (data available on the Defra website). In consequence, the net worth of the farming industry – asset values less liabilities – has risen steadily at a cumulative rate of almost 6 per cent per year, making landowners – two-thirds of farmers own their own land – asset rich if cash poor.

According to government figures (ibid.) the industry's net worth is estimated to have been £102 billion in 2003. This should

Figure 2   **Real per capita farming income**

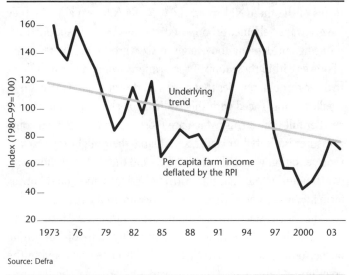

Source: Defra

be set against the knowledge that some 85 per cent of the industry's value-added is generated by just 20 per cent of the UK's 304,800 farm holdings (ibid.). As many larger farm businesses own more than one holding this suggests – there are no official data on farm businesses – that the capitalised value of farm support is concentrated in 50,000 or fewer farm businesses. These farm businesses tend to be large-scale and generally more productive and efficient than their smaller counterparts. They also dominate the councils and committees of the three NFUs and the CLA. This is inevitable given the fact that to fully engage as a council and/or committee member a farmer must be able to delegate the running of their farms for a significant number of days per year to employees or family members.

The dominance of larger-scale farmers in the policy mechanisms of the three NFUs and the CLA helps to explain why they have always vehemently opposed the modulation support. i.e. reducing entitlement above a given size threshold. The structure of power within these lobby organisations would make it difficult to drive through policies that positively discriminated in favour of smaller farms. Faced with this reality it has become common for smaller full-time farms, which are most vulnerable to the income pressures indicated in Figure 2, to blame their plight on a lack of representation within the three NFUs and the CLA. It is, however, worth pointing out that this criticism seriously took hold only as farm incomes came under extreme pressure in the 1990s.

The dissatisfaction of smaller-scale farms has resulted in NFU members accounting for a diminishing share of a declining farmer population. Dissatisfaction has also been reflected in the creation of a number of alternative lobby groups. The first was the Tenant Farmers Association in the early 1980s, and this has been followed in the 1990s by the Small Farms Association, the Family Farms Association and, more recently, Farmers for Action (FFA). A reading of the information published on these organisations' websites show that they have in common a belief that the current agricultural policy, and by implication the three NFUs and the CLA, is oriented towards industrialised farming and consequently the marginalisation of smaller-scale, higher-cost producers. Ironically, in creating rival farm lobbies they also serve to further weaken the power of the farm lobby per se by providing the government with greater scope to play one interest off against another.

The external influence

Coleman and Tangermann (1999) show that within the EU agricultural policy is increasingly being shaped by international policy-making, in particular multilateral trade negotiations and EU enlargement. The MacSharry reform of 1992 reflected the ascendancy (if modestly) of market liberalisation over protectionism: it began the process of dismantling open-ended price support and replacing it with more transparent direct payments. For the professional advisers within the NFU it was manifest that the pursuit of freer trade would henceforth take precedence over trade-distorting protection. Such a move was bound to reduce farm incomes and it provoked a new realism within the three NFUs and the CLA.

The three NFUs and the CLA were already on the defensive. Agricultural surpluses and the high cost of their disposal on to world markets had effectively ended the corporatist bargain forged between the state and the three NFUs to expand agricultural production (Cox et al., 1988). Moreover, an articulate environmental lobby had made considerable progress in persuading public opinion that instead of rural stewardship modern industrialised farming brought with it environmental damage, animal welfare issues and food scares (Buller and Morris, 2003). In consequence, the three NFUs and the CLA found that their traditional position of authority on rural matters was coming under increasing threat (Halfacree, 1999).

The outcome was a marked change in the role and policies of the three NFUs and the CLA. The introduction of business services to their members offered scope to offset the pressures on subscriptions of falling membership, but it was also tacit recognition that in future governments would be less helpful. In 1992 the

NFU of England and Wales set up NFU Services to provide advice and consultancy, and following in a similar direction the CLA changed its full title to the Country Landowners' and Business Association in 2001. On the policy front, by the early 1990s both organisations were giving the environment a higher status in their policy-making; for example, the NFU of England and Wales set up a department dedicated to environmental policy.

Although membership of the three NFUs and the CLA is in decline, there is no evidence that membership of the smaller/ tenanted farm organisation is growing. These organisations, along with FFA, are very coy when it comes to revealing precise membership numbers, but it is very unlikely that any of these organisations could show an active membership in excess of 10,000. If, however, these smaller farm lobbies lacked the professionalism and 'insider' intelligence of the three NFUs and the CLA, they could at least take comfort from the support they attracted from the now more powerful environmental lobby. The growing emphasis on ecological sustainability was changing the balance between farm and environmental lobbies and their respective abilities to influence policy.

At the start of the 1990s the NFU of England and Wales perceived the changing policy environment and in a policy document setting out its longer-term perspective it explicitly switched the justification for farm support from expanding production to the role of farmers as 'custodians of the countryside' (NFU, 1994). During the 1990s this line of thought within the EU gave rise to the concept of 'multi-functionality': an acknowledgement that farming produces a host of public goods such as the management of the rural landscape and ecology and by implication their provision deserves public support. Thus, by the mid-

Figure 3   **Alternative futures**

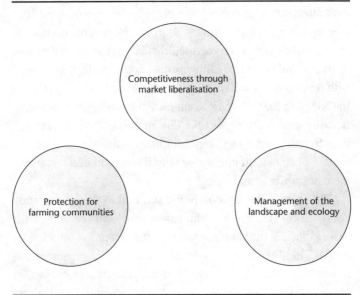

1990s it was possible to identify the three different possible futures for the evolution of EU agricultural policy as set out in Figure 3. The problem for the farm lobby was that they constituted an irreconcilable trinity.

The British government was in the vanguard of those member states pushing for greater market liberalisation, and at home it had signalled an interest in modernising rural policy which was to result in a Rural White Paper in 2000 (Lowe et al., 2002). The NFU of England and Wales, recognising the value of its 'insider' status, concluded that it could achieve more by working with, rather than opposing, the direction of flow. The NFU's realpolitik reason for changing its policy stance so as to more closely align it with the government's objectives was the recognition that the impending multilateral trade agreement (the Uruguay Agreement) would not seek to reduce payments to agriculture for the purpose of environmental policies. It also recognised that large transparent income transfers could be more easily justified domestically if associated with provision of a well-managed countryside (NFU, 1994). Thus the NFU and the CLA came to embrace the concept of multi-functionality in order to protect the flow of public funds to farming, but they hoped to use their combined influence to limit the burden of regulation implied by official direction of the management of landscape and ecology.

The three-'pillar' approach first surfaced in the 1999 Agenda 2000 reform (European Commission, 1997), but became much more explicit in the latest Fischler reform (European Commission, 2002). The Agenda 2000 reform acknowledged, if not wholeheartedly embraced, the concept of subsidiarity and opened up opportunities for individual member states to tailor CAP regimes to meet national priorities and circumstances, and the Fischler reform has taken the process further. Returning some discretion in agricultural policy to national, and indeed regional, governments has to some extent revived the 'insider' status of the three NFUs and the CLA. But as if to demonstrate the waning power of the farm lobby, in implementing the Fischler reform in England the NFU was unable to prevent the single farm payment being progressively introduced on a flat-rate basis, thereby effectively redistributing support from highly productive to less productive farms.

Internal challenges

While the three NFUs have continued to pursue their 'insider' status, a number of farmers – the evidence suggests generally smaller, full-time farmers – have lost patience and have chosen to seek to achieve their objectives by militancy. Direct activism is the *raison d'être* of the FFA (Woods, 2004), though as noted above its active membership probably amounts to significantly less than 10,000 and in terms of a public profile it is associated with its founder, David Handley. Started in 2000 as real farm incomes reached a post-war low (see Figure 2), the FFA has chosen, after a flirtation with fuel taxes, to target its direct actions at the supermarkets, which, it believes, have the power to raise prices and ensure that the additional revenue is passed back to farmers.

The FFA stance is again implicit recognition that increased levels of support will not be forthcoming from the government. It is significant, however, that the FFA have concentrated their efforts on milk prices, where there is a clearly defined product, limited substitutes, a short supply chain and a relatively smaller number of downstream players. The FFA has made very little impression in other sectors. At first it appeared to have some success in raising the milk price, but the benefits were short lived. The easing of the economic pressures on farming – a change that owes all to a weakening of the pound against the euro – and the prospects of some redistribution of support towards smaller-scale farms following the Fischler reform have probably drawn the FFA's sting and its longer-term existence must now be in doubt.

Looking forward, the Countryside Alliance (CA) has emerged as a threat to the three NFUs and the CLA. Created in 1997 to oppose the anticipated ban on hunting with dogs, the CA has attempted to widen its remit to that of a countryside movement.

The CA was helped in this respect by the coincidence of its founding and the deepening income crisis in farming. It was able to capitalise on this crisis (and other rural concerns) with the effect that it attracted very large numbers from rural communities on its marches, in the process placing itself in the vanguard of protecting rural communities. The CA claims to campaign for the countryside, country sports and the rural way of life, including food and farming (CA website). Whether prompted by the CA or not, the farm lobby has now moved to occupy this area.

The three NFUs and the CLA have, since the mid-1990s, sought to position themselves as representing a wider constituency than just farms. For example, the NFU of England and Wales introduced a new category of countryside membership in the early 1990s, and members in this category now outnumber full-farmer members. Again, it is too early to judge whether the CA will grow to a size whereby it threatens the survival of the three NFUs and the CLA. If the CA is to reach this position it will have to build a much more effective and therefore expensive regional network. As the farmer lobby has discovered, relying solely on farmer subscriptions to finance such a network is a constant struggle to remain financially viable. In July 2003 the NFU announced that in future it would work more closely with the CLA and would move its headquarters out of London. An amalgamation with the CLA was considered, but rejected on cost grounds. In these actions it is, however, possible to envision, at some point in the future, a single countryside organisation or federation to represent the interests of not only farmers but also a wider range of businesses working in rural areas.

Concluding thoughts

The three NFUs remain a powerful force. This was demonstrated during the 2001 outbreak of foot-and-mouth disease, when they became the farmers' main source of advice and used their skills to secure very generous compensation for farmers. But the re-election of the Labour government in the same year saw the Ministry of Agriculture, Fisheries and Food absorbed into the Department for Environment, Food and Rural Affairs. The change made explicit the ascendancy of rural and environmental policies over farming policies in the government's view. It remains true that expenditure on agricultural policies is many times greater than expenditure on environmental and rural policies, but the farm lobby's professional advisers know that the future holds only a redistribution of agricultural expenditure towards the provision of environmental public goods. In working to ensure that farms will remain the major recipients of public funding, the farm lobby is becoming more of a rural business and environment lobby.

References

Buller, H. and C. Morris (2003), 'Farm animal welfare: a new repertoire of nature–society relations or modernism embedded?', *Sociologia Ruralis*, 43.

Coleman, D. and S. Tangermann (1999), *The 1992 CAP Reform, the Uruguay Round and the Commission: Conceptualising linked policy games*, vol. 37–3, pp. 385–405.

Cox, G., P. Lowe and M. Winter (1988), 'Private rights and public responsibilities: the prospects for agricultural and environmental controls', *Journal of Rural Studies*, 4.

Defra (2005), *Agriculture in the UK*, London.

European Commission (1997), *Agenda 2000: For a stronger and wider Europe*, Brussels.

European Commission (2002), *Communication on the Mid-term Review: Towards sustainable farming*, Brussels.

Grant, W. (1983), 'The National Farmers' Union: the classic case of incorporation in pressure politics', in D. Marsh (ed.), *Interest Groups in Britain*, London: Junction Books.

Halfacree, K. (1999), 'A new space or spatial effacement? Alternative futures for the post-productivist countryside', in N. Walford, J. Everitt and D. Napton (eds), *Reshaping the Countryside: Perceptions and processes of rural change*, Wallingford: CAB International.

Lowe, F., H. Buller and N. Ward (2002), 'Setting the next agenda? British and French approaches to the second pillar of the Common Agricultural Policy', *Journal of Rural Studies*, 18.

NFU (1994), *Real Choices*, London: National Farmers' Union.

Rickard, S. (2000), 'British farming: time for a new mindset', *Journal of the Royal Agricultural Society*.

Rickard, S. (2004), 'CAP reform, competitiveness and sustainability', *Journal of the Science of Food and Agriculture*, 84.

Winter, L. (1989), 'The so-called non-economic objectives of agricultural policy', *OECD Economic Studies*, 13.

Woods, M. (2004), 'Politics and protests in the contemporary countryside', in L. Holloway and M. Kneafsey (eds), *Geographies of Rural Cultures and Societies*, London: Ashgate.

11 UK FORESTRY – A LOST OPPORTUNITY
Barry Gamble

Introduction

Forests comprise almost 10 per cent of non-urban and non-agricultural land in the UK. But few would be clear about the aesthetic, environmental or economic contributions that this substantial land use makes.

Ever since the much-publicised withdrawal of tax relief for new forestry planting in 1988 the UK industry has been directionless. Reasons cited include continual reductions in grant aid, a collapse in timber prices, increased recycling, regulation, the strength of sterling and overseas competition.

This article argues that the problems in the UK forest industry stem largely from its structure. If this issue were addressed, forestry could play a much greater role in the UK rural economy.

The Forestry Commission

Almost half the total forest area in the UK is under the umbrella of the state-run Forestry Commission (FC). Up until now the state has also supplied rather more than half the total volume of timber to the market from its more mature estate.

The FC was founded in 1919, before the British Broadcasting Corporation or the Milk Marketing Board, with the primary objective of producing a strategic reserve of timber, through the creation of state forests and the encouragement of private sector planting.

The stated aim of the FC is 'the sustainable management of our existing woods and forests and a steady expansion of tree cover to increase the many, diverse benefits that forests provide to meet the needs of present and future generations'. The FC also has roles in undertaking forest research and protecting plant health.

From the 1950s, the role of forestry was increasingly interpreted in terms of reducing reliance on imports and stimulating the rural economy. Subsequently the quality of the landscape and wildlife habitats started to become important factors.

The multi-tasking role of the FC as adviser to government on forestry policy, industry regulator, loss-making and market-dominant commercial operator and, probably, the timber seller of last resort runs counter to the interests of all woodland owners, whether public or private.

A number of commentators have made the point that there are no comparable organisations with such diverse and conflicting roles. I believe that this structure is a barrier to the successful development of the forest industry.

Timber markets

The UK is one of the best places in the world to grow softwood timber and one of the world's largest timber consumers. UK timber prices have fallen consistently since 1996, however, and, in real terms, home-grown timber is cheaper than ever before.

We believe that the main causes are a direct result of government policies acting through the FC.

- The government has paid direct and indirect grants to wood processors to replace sustainable sources of timber with recycled fibre. This has dramatically reduced the market for sawmilling co-products (sawdust, offcuts, bark) and the lower grades of timber within the pulp and paper and wood-based panel industries. As a consequence, best-management woodland practices are compromised both economically and environmentally.
- The state-owned Forest Enterprise (the commercial arm of the Foresty Commission) has increasingly acted as the 'timber supplier of last resort', always being prepared to supply timber at the margin. Does this have competition or fair trading implications?
- The government has for some years failed to attract new timber processing industry, despite the obvious economic benefits that this could bring both to rural communities and to deprived urban areas. The scale of investment required in building large-scale processing, such as paper mills, means that government involvement is important. Such investment is required to replace the capacity lost to recycled fibre and to deal with the increasing availability of timber from forests planted during the 1970s and 1980s.
- Rather than investing in rural transport infrastructure, local authorities have been permitted to prevent timber lorries from using public roads. In some cases this has effectively 'landlocked' properties. This is particularly inequitable given the high burden of road tax and fuel duty paid for by the haulage industry.

As a consequence of low UK timber prices, unprocessed

timber is exported to Finland, Sweden and Ireland to supply their well-developed industries.

At the same time, the rate of new planting has collapsed from a steady 30,000 hectares per year in the 1970s and 1980s to just 13,500 hectares in 2003, of which only around 30 per cent comprises commercial species. The reason is simple. The agricultural sector still holds real political muscle, obtaining £160 per hectare per annum in government support. In contrast, private sector forests, despite the high level of public benefits, receive a mere £18 per hectare. The large-scale conifer forests owned by the FC cost the state some £92 per hectare per annum. Subsidies inevitably distort markets with substantial direct and indirect costs to the whole supply chain. The distorting effect of subsidies can be more effectively eradicated by ending subsidies to all sectors.

Although the forestry sector has attempted to organise a cohesive response with the 'A level playing field for forestry' campaign, the effectiveness of this campaign has been watered down by powerful establishment interests.

As an adviser to government, the FC has failed the forest industry. More importantly, rural communities have been denied a viable economic alternative to agriculture, which could have increased the economic, social, visual and biological diversity of many rural areas.

Industry regulation

The FC also profoundly influences the development of the forest industry by the way in which it regulates the industry. It does this through a combination of controls on harvesting and the issuing of grants for specific operations. The guiding principle is one of 'sustainability', which is defined by the UK Woodland Assurance Scheme.

The concept of sustainability is fully accepted within the industry, but it is here that differences begin to emerge. The FC, rather predictably, uses a much more prescriptive and bureaucratic approach than the private sector considers appropriate and tends to elevate the role of landscape design. The FC also missed a major point when it failed to ensure that meeting grant criteria also achieved certification status. As a result we have unnecessary regulation.

The real impact on the development of sustainable forestry is in the grant structures and their application. The government has specific objectives and is prepared to pay for them. For example, the government wants to establish native woodlands and to encourage public access to woods.

Theoretically, the FC should pay a set rate for achieving these objectives – owners could, for example, be paid per hectare of native woodland created. When criteria are complex, the owners could bid for funds, to be considered against other potential applicants according to published measures.

Given stability, scale and clear objectives, such an approach would encourage the development of rural entrepreneurs, who would constantly develop more efficient ways to meet public benefits. There would be great potential for such an approach to play an important role in rural renewal. Unfortunately, the increasing complexity of the FC grant systems and their reliance on standard costing approaches deter any innovation.

Even those who manage to qualify for the grants still might not get paid. For example, in 2004 the FC ran short of cash in England. Predictably, it alleviated the problem by stopping grant payments.

If this were not enough of a deterrent, then the threat of 'further consultation' can kill any enthusiasm. The complexity, costs and endless 'talking shops' act as an additional brake on the development of an effective forest industry and increase the cost to the taxpayer of purchasing public benefits.

Market drivers

The FC is Britain's largest landowner and manages some 800,000 hectares of forest, of which some 89 per cent comprise conifers, compared to a more balanced 46 per cent in the private sector. As a result, the FC accounts for some 62 per cent of UK softwood production, which allows it to dominate the market.

Research carried out by fountains plc into the UK timber market analysed the behaviour of the FC and discovered a strong *negative* correlation between the volume of timber harvested by the FC and prevailing timber prices. As timber prices begin to fall, it appears that the FC responds by increasing its harvest, so that a fixed revenue target can be achieved.

By supplying the market with timber when prices are low, but reducing the harvest when prices increase, the FC increases the volatility in timber prices. Such volatility deters investment in new processing capacity as well as in the growing sector, in what is a 'lose-lose' relationship between the grower and the processor.

Although such a strategy may generate cash flow, it destroys value as the timber is sold significantly below its cost of production. In fact, the FC incurred a trading loss of £74 million following this strategy in 2004, equivalent to £92 per hectare. After forest asset revaluations, losses increased to over £300 million. Such a figure hardly has the ring of sustainability.

Such calculations expose the lie that the FC can act as an example to the private sector. One would expect the FC to benefit from economies of scale. Since the FC has large, mature conifer forests and the private sector has a large number of small woodlands, including a much higher proportion of broadleaves, then why is it that it costs the FC five times as much per hectare to maintain its assets as it costs the private sector?

Surely the private sector, given the scale of the FC, could do much, much better. Forestry has significant economies of scale, and by clinging on to the management of such a high proportion of commercial forestry, the private sector is denied a further opportunity to develop.

In countries such as the USA, New Zealand and Australia forestry has developed into an asset class of its own, which is widely used as part of investment portfolios. If this is to develop in the UK, it is essential that the forest industry increases its scale. This would also drive down costs through the wood supply chain to create an internationally competitive processing industry, benefiting both timber growers and processors.

International comparisons
New forestry planting

The continuing requirement for planting grants brings into question the viability of new forestry planting. Those planning new planting must implicitly assume that the timber price experience of the last ten years would not form the basis of determining final crop revenues at the end of the rotation. The continuing requirement for grant reintroduces the question of how well timber markets operate in this country and the persuasive influence of the FC in this respect. Nonetheless, some investors are prepared to consider planting without the availability of grants and find the process less inhibiting, cumbersome and time consuming.

Through its regulatory role of administering grant aid for planting, the FC by its actions is probably inhibiting increased levels of forestry planting. The FC has a finite pool from which to pay grants. This restricts the volume of new planting, the demand for plants from nurseries and the wider benefits that might emerge from a more high-volume approach.

We might speculate what might happen if forestry planting grants were reduced or were even non-existent and the bureaucracy surrounding planting applications removed. This might act as a spur to draw more significant volumes through the nurseries, stimulating more competitive pricing for plants and the costs of planting. The current grant mechanisms just might be a particularly expensive way of achieving woodland cover.

An interesting international comparison is between the UK and New Zealand. In the 1970s the forestry industry in both countries was structured along similar lines. Since that period, however, the countries have diverged, particularly in terms of the role of the state in the forestry industry.

Following the formation of the New Zealand Forest Service in 1919, the New Zealand forestry industry followed a similar model to that in the UK, with the New Zealand Forest Service responsible for implementing multi-objective forestry and owning 52 per cent of the forest estate.

During the 1980s, a number of factors caused the government to rethink the way in which it managed its forests. These included:

- the need to encourage expansion of the timber processing industry to absorb the increasing timber supply;
- an increasing emphasis on sustainable forest management;
- a wider government economic policy of industry deregulation to improve competitiveness;
- a desire within government to clarify organisational objectives to enable transparency and accountability.

As a result, in 1987 the roles of the New Zealand Forest Service were split as follows:

- New Zealand Forestry Corporation (NZFC) – tasked with managing the state's commercial forestry for a profit.
- Department of Conservation – tasked with management of natural forests.
- Ministry of Forestry – tasked with policy, forest health, protection and research.

Although the split appeared to be an improvement, it was considered that the change did not go far enough, for the following reasons:

- A central part of government policy was economic reform to improve the international competitiveness of New Zealand industry.
- The state-ownership status of NZFC could allow political interference.
- The processing sector could be constrained by NZFC. The ability of the processing sector to purchase its own forests for long-term timber supply was constrained.

- The transfer value of the forests from the state to the NZFC could not be agreed.

Because of this, a large-scale privatisation programme began in 1990 and was completed by 1996. The state now owns less than 7 per cent of the planted forest area, with most being owned by foreign investors. It is interesting to note that a number of other countries have followed a similar approach, or are considering doing so. These include countries as diverse as Malawi, Ghana and Romania.

The reforms carried out in the late 1980s resulted in several years of real hardship, particularly for the sawmilling sector, with many smaller mills closing. Timber production stagnated between 1984 and 1989 and afforestation fell from a peak of around 55,000 hectares to some 15,000 hectares per annum.

The sector was forced to focus on areas of true competitive advantage, and this meant that the industry emerged as a leaner and fitter competitor. Investment in processing capacity increased from NZD 11 million in 1988 to an average annual level of NZD 165 million by 2002. At the same time timber production more than doubled and afforestation reached a new peak of 95,000 hectares in the mid-1990s.

The way forward

The FC's remit is clearly no longer appropriate for today's world. It is just not tenable that it should have so many roles and responsibilities. The FC has even publicly stated that it had 'some sympathy with ... concern over the multi tasking role ... as adviser to the government on policy, as a regulator and as a commercial operator ... there is no doubt more we can do ...'

In what other sector would we have an organisation that is adviser to government on forestry policy, regulator and dominant commercial operator? In aviation terms, the equivalent would be the Department for Transport, the Civil Aviation Authority, the British Airports Authority, British Airways, Ryanair and easyJet all operating as a single organisation. This might leave Sir Michael Bishop of British Midland representing the private commercial sector.

In such a multi-tasking organisation, where would be the transparency, the accountability, the corporate governance?

It matters not whether Forest Enterprise is owned by the state or privately. What matters is its positioning. What is important is its influence over policy, its intimacy with the regulator and its dominance in the timber marketplace. FE properties should be managed in the same market, under the same regulatory and sustainability criteria, as those of the private sector. Multi-purpose forestry should no longer be used as a front for lack of transparency and accountability.

UK forestry does not have to be a depressed sector, but with timber prices at such low levels it is hard for those within the industry to conceive of any better situation. By contrast, in a number of countries around the world forestry is undergoing something of a renaissance, making a valuable contribution to the economy and the environment. Forestry investment groups and conservation groups have learnt how to work in partnership.

Financial institutions have also recognised the attractions of forestry as a long-term investment asset. Approaching $20 billion has been invested in the sector by pension funds and other long-term investors in a range of countries such as Argentina, Australia,

Brazil, Canada, Chile, New Zealand and the USA. One of the most recent high-profile transactions is a long-term investment in forestry by the Harvard endowment of some $600 million. Such a level of investment would just about meet the most recent annual losses of the state-run Forestry Commission here.

We need to redirect the impact of public sector forestry, which has simply become too detached from the real considerations affecting private woodland owners.

So what should be done? The industry needs a regulator, independent of the Forestry Commission, a body able to regulate both public and private sector in exactly the same way. In many respects the industry is well capable of self-regulation with forests managed to independently recognised sustainability criteria, such as those of the Forest Stewardship Council. What is clear is that we don't need two contradicting layers of regulation as at present, first under certification and then under compliance with FC grant regulations.

We should then move on to identify in the public sector forest estate those properties that have particularly high amenity, wildlife or other environmental value. These properties should be placed into new 'national forests'. The National Forest in the English Midlands has been an important policy success and would provide an ideal model.

The remaining Forest Enterprise properties would be placed into regional commercial corporations, which would operate to the same market and regulatory constraints as the private sector.

For the private owner this new structure would bring transparency and visibility to the regulatory and operational framework. These corporations might be able to raise external private capital, recognising the government's keenness for public/private partnership. New capital invested in growing and managing trees could well help lower the cost of or redirect Common Agricultural Policy funding, with land being diverted from agriculture.

Without such a change, the Forestry Commission will continue as an ongoing financial drain on the Treasury, and the private sector will fail to realise any of the potential being seen in so many overseas markets at this time.

We have lost sight of what forestry is all about because of the way in which the Forestry Commission has dominated forestry thinking for so long. An asset base valued at several hundred million pounds should surely be capable of generating a positive return to both public and private sector owners. The Post Office has been turned from loss to profit; what is so different about the forestry industry?

12 SUNSETS, SUBJECTIVE VALUE, THE ENVIRONMENT AND THE ENGLISH COUNTRYSIDE
Julian Morris

At sunset on a clear summer's day, the view to the west from my parents' house is always stunning: London ensconced in a beautiful orange glow, the result of the sun's late afternoon rays diffracting through the capital's hazy atmosphere. I have often wondered what value my parents and their neighbours in South Essex put on this vista, so humbly maintained by industrialists and vehicle users.

Those individuals living along London's clogged arteries no doubt have a different view of these emissions. One might speculate that many of these people would be happier if they had a little less ozone with their breakfast. But, of course, we must not forget the industrialists and vehicle users who benefit directly from their haze-producing activities.

With so many different interests at stake, what is the best way to decide how much haze to allow? Two popular views are those espoused by 'environmentalists' and 'economists'.[1] The standard environmentalist response is to demand regulations that would drastically limit emissions by vehicles and industry. In contrast, the standard economist response is to identify the 'socially

---

1   The discussion here presents something of a caricature of what economists and environmentalists tend to say about the subject. The author applauds those environmentalists and economists who object to this caricature and hopes they will encourage others to think less narrowly.

optimal' level of emissions and construct a rational system of taxes and tradable permits that would lead to this outcome in an efficient manner. Both 'solutions' are problematic.

The environmentalist response presumes that all emissions are harmful and that there are essentially no beneficial effects arising from industry and vehicle use, even at the margin.[2] To the environmentalist, the optimal level of emissions is zero.

The economist response is in many ways more reasonable than that of the environmentalist. It is unlikely that all members of society, even a simple majority, would want to eliminate emissions altogether (at least, not if it involves increased costs or reduced income). Even those who favour significant reductions in emissions in some places might think that emissions in other places (for example, in places where no person is adversely affected) would be perfectly acceptable. But the economist's solution begins with the assumption that it is possible to achieve the 'optimal' level of emissions through the actions of an all-powerful central regulator.[3] Given the subjective nature of desires (as exemplified above by the aesthetes who appreciate man-made sunsets), it is not even possible for the state to identify the 'optimal' level of pollution, let

2   To extremist environmentalists, the orange haze would, by virtue of its unnatural origin, be condemned as aesthetically undesirable.

3   For example, the economists might try to conduct surveys to establish each householder's willingness to pay for cleaner air or better sunsets. The evidence suggests, however, that the numbers would be of little merit. The best that could be hoped for is that the surveys would rank the importance individuals and groups attach to various concerns. See, e.g., Coursey (1997); Kahneman and Knetch (1992). The problem with such surveys, at base, is that they do not, indeed cannot, replicate the mental processes that occur when a person makes a decision to buy or sell a good – so the values they obtain are not 'prices'. For an explanation of how prices arise and their function in coordinating economic activity, see Hayek (1945).

alone construct laws that will bring this optimum about.[4]

The problem is a little like that faced by a heating engineer attempting to ensure that each room of a house is at the right temperature. The first houses with central heating typically had one thermostat that would govern when the heating was on or off. The problem was that each room had different thermal properties – some had big windows, others small windows; some had high ceilings, others low ceilings. So – especially when doors were closed – the thermostat would ensure that the room in which it was placed was kept at the 'right' temperature, while most other rooms would be too hot or too cold. Heating engineers have since realised that the best way to enable each room to be kept at the optimal temperature is to put individual thermostats in each room or on each radiator. And so it is with the preferences for environmental quality.

Just as decentralisation of temperature control results in better, more effective temperature management, a growing body of scholarly literature suggests that many environmental amenities may be provided more effectively, and in a way that better enables individuals to achieve their goals, through decentralised institutions rather than through central government intervention.[5]

4   The economist solution also typically ignores – or intentionally avoids – the issue of compensating losers. The standard by which actions are judged by such economists is 'potential Pareto optimality', under which it is enough that the winners *could* compensate the losers, not that they would actually so do. Baumol and Oates (1988); see also Sagoff (1994). So, in the above example, if the central authority decides that the householders in Essex gain more from particulate pollution than Londoners lose, then it is sufficient that the Essex folk could in principle compensate the Londoners. (The main argument used in favour of this standard is that it obviates the problem of transaction costs associated with both the collection of revenue from beneficiaries and their disbursement to losers.)

5   Such literature can be traced back at least to Coase (1960), which critiques the unilateral nature of the 'externality' as conceptualised in particular by Arthur

Common-law liability for environmental damage,[6] combined with contracts,[7] easements and covenants[8] would, this literature suggests, in many if not most cases be more effective in providing the kinds of environmental amenities that people actually want.

Nuisance law and environmental protection

This article focuses primarily on the role of private nuisance law – a branch of law that has traditionally dealt with ongoing interferences with private property.[9] The nuisance action emerged in the Middle Ages as a means of protecting the rights of landowners to use and enjoy their property free from interference by others. In 1443, Judge Markam clarified what sorts of interference were actionable: 'if a man builds a house and stops up the light coming to my house, or causes rain to fall from his house and so undermines my house, or does anything which injures my free tenement, I shall have the assize of nuisance' (Coquillette, 1979: 770).

In 1608, William Aldred brought an action at the Norfolk Assizes concerning a pigsty built by his neighbour, Thomas Benton. The pigsty was adjacent to Aldred's house and had

---

Pigou. Coase (ibid.:.18) argues that externalities are 'reciprocal' and is concerned that the unilateral theory espoused by Pigou serves to promote an unjustified view of the role of the state in correcting market 'defects': 'It is my belief that economists, and policy-makers generally, have tended to overestimate the advantages which come from government regulation.'

6   See, e.g., Coase (1960), who shows that liability rules affect the structure of property rights; see also Calabresi and Melamed (1972); Littlechild (1979); Cheung (1978); Macaulay (1991); Yandle, (1997).

7   In principle all amenities could be provided through contract. See Pennington (2002).

8   Ellickson (1973).

9   The following discussion draws extensively on Brenner (1973); Ogus and Richardson (1977); Coquillette (1979) and McLaren (1983).

created a stink. Benton argued in his defence that 'the building of the house for hogs was necessary for the sustenance of man, and one ought not to have so delicate a nose, that he cannot bear the smell of hogs'.[10] This attempt to use a 'public benefit' argument failed, however, and the judge ruled in Aldred's favour.

Sir Edward Coke employed Aldred's case to clarify the rule of nuisance: property holders were entitled to use and enjoy their property free from interference, but the extent of this right was only that of ordinary comfort and necessity, not delicate taste.[11] Once it had been established that a right had been breached, no putative 'public benefit' would justify the *damnum*. Here, Coke employed the Roman maxim *sic utere tuo ut alienum non laedas* (so use your own property as not to injure your neighbours).[12] The *sic utere* rule was employed in numerous seventeenth-century cases,[13] and was famously restated by Lord Holt in the 1704 case of *Tennant* v. *Goldwin*:[14] Goldwin had failed to maintain an adjoining wall, causing a stink from his privy to enter Tennant's house, which affected Tennant's enjoyment of his property. Lord Holt, finding for Tennant, concluded, 'And as every man is bound so to look to his cattle, as to keep them out of his neighbour's ground ... so he must keep in the filth of his house or office, that it may not flow in upon and damnify his neighbour.'

Blackstone's affirmative expression of the *sic utere tuo* rule

---

10   *Aldred's Case* (1611).
11   'In a house four things are desired [habitation of man, pleasure of the inhabitant, necessity of light, and cleanliness of air], and for nuisance done to three of them an action lies' (ibid.).
12   Ibid.
13   These included *Jones* v. *Powell* (1628), *Morley* v. *Pragnel* (1638) and *Tuberville* v. *Stam* (1697).
14   *Tennant* v. *Goldwin* (1705).

suggests that through the mid-eighteenth century it held sway and was commonly applied to harms that have a distinctly modern environmental feel to them:

> [I]f one erects a smelting house for lead so near the land of another that the vapour and smoke kills his corn and grass, and damages his cattle therein, this is held to be a nuisance … [I]f one does any other act, in itself lawful, which yet being done in that place necessarily tends to the damage of another's property, it is a nuisance: for it is incumbent on him to find some other place to do that act where it will be less offensive.[15]

Prescriptive easements: acquiring the right to pollute by prior appropriation

While *sic utere tuo* was the rule, there were exceptions. In the 1791 case of *R* v. *Neville*,[16] the British Crown brought a case in public nuisance[17] against a 'maker of kitchen stuff and other grease' for fouling the air. But Neville had been carrying on his trade for some time without objection from his neighbours and Lord Kenyon advised the jury that 'where manufacturers have been borne within a neighbourhood for many years, it will operate as a consent of the inhabitants to their being carried on, though the law might have considered them as nuisances, had they been

---

15 Blackstone (n.d.: 217–18).

16 *R* v. *Neville* (1791).

17 The public nuisance is a separate action to the private nuisance. It relates to harms to the general public and is primarily enforced by the Crown, although individuals may also argue a case in public nuisance if the extent of harm they suffer is greater than that suffered by other members of the public.

objected to in time'.[18] The jury acquitted the defendant. Following this reasoning, a person may acquire a prescriptive right to cause harm to neighbouring properties even though, if actioned, the harms would be considered a nuisance.

In his ruing in *R* v. *Neville*, Lord Kenyon observed that the consent to pollute would not apply to a newcomer who made the air 'very disagreeable and uncomfortable'. So, while a newcomer whose actions made only a marginal difference to air quality would not be liable for their portion of the harm caused to neighbouring properties,[19] a newcomer whose actions made the air substantially worse could still be held liable.

This rule (developed in a public nuisance case) was affirmed but constrained in the 1838 (private nuisance) case of *Bliss* v. *Hale*,[20] in which a plaintiff complained of noxious smells and vapours arising from the works of a tallow chandler, which allegedly interfered with the plaintiff's beneficial use of his property. The court ruled that since the defendant had been causing the nuisance for only three years, he had not acquired a prescriptive easement to continue, for which at least twenty years' continuous operation would have been necessary. In *Sturges* v. *Bridgeman*,[21] the courts made clear that the harm itself, not merely the action causing the harm, must have continued for a period of twenty years in order for a right to have been acquired by prescription. This case was eloquently described by Ronald Coase:

> In this case, a confectioner ... used two mortars and pestles in connection with his business (one had been in operation

18   *R* v. *Neville* (1791).
19   Ibid.
20   *Bliss* v. *Hale* (1838).
21   *Sturges* v. *Bridgeman* (1879).

in the same position for more than 60 years and the other for more than 26 years). A doctor then came to occupy neighbouring premises. … The confectioner's machinery caused the doctor no harm until, eight years after he had first occupied the premises [that is, 34 years after the youngest pestle and mortar was first put into operation], he built a consulting room at the end of his garden right against the confectioner's kitchen. It was then found that the noise and vibration caused by the confectioner's machinery made it difficult for the doctor to use his new consulting room. … The doctor therefore brought a legal action to force the confectioner to stop using his machinery. (Coase, 1960: 8–9)

The courts, granting an injunction to the doctor, remarked:

Whether anything is to be considered a nuisance or not is a question to be determined not merely by an abstract consideration of the thing itself, but in reference to its circumstances. What would be a nuisance in Belgrave Square [then and now a high-class residential district in London's West End] would not necessarily be so in Bermondsey [an area on the south side of the Thames, then full of tanneries].[22]

The law was clarified further in *St Helen's Smelting Co.* v. *Tipping*, where a distinction was drawn between interference with property and interference with peaceful enjoyment. In 1859, Mr Tipping purchased a 1,300-acre estate near St Helen's in Merseyside. Four years later he brought an action against the St Helen's Smelting Company, alleging that their nearby copper smelting works had (1) caused injury to trees, hedges, fruit and cattle on

22   Ibid.

his land, and (2) caused substantial personal discomfort.[23] The judge in the lower court instructed the jury that the law was not concerned with 'trifling inconveniences' and that where noxious vapours were concerned 'the injury to be actionable must be such as visibly to diminish the value of the property and the comfort and enjoyment of it'. The jury awarded damages of £361 to Tipping. The Lords upheld the judgment but qualified it by clearly distinguishing between damage to the property itself, which would be actionable regardless of where the property was located, and interference with the beneficial use of that property, which would depend on the location of the property (and in this case was not available because of the industrial setting).

Although the rule in nuisance law remained *sic utere tuo*, its interpretation, and specifically whether there can be said to be *damnum*, in any case would depend on the type of interference that was alleged. Nuisance was effectively split into two separate torts:

- Tangible nuisance: If there were physical harm to property (for example, damage to trees and shrubs) then it would be necessary only to show that the harm had been caused by the defendant's action and that some kind of harm was a foreseeable consequence of the defendant's action. In *Fletcher* v. *Rylands*, the defendant had constructed a reservoir on his property in order to power his mill, but the water escaped into the plaintiff's mine shaft, causing severe damage. Judge Blackburn in the lower court asserted 'that the person who for his own purposes brings on his lands and collects and

---

23   *St Helen's Smelting Co.* v. *Tipping* (1865), p. 865.

keeps there anything likely to do mischief if it escapes, must keep it in at his peril'.[24] The result was to reaffirm the general principle of *sic utere tuo*: if a defendant uses his property in such a way that it might cause harm to another's and if some harm in fact materialises, then the defendant should be liable for the harm (for ongoing instances of physical interference there would of course be no need to show foreseeability).

- Intangible nuisance: For interference with property that does not result in physical injury to the property itself (for example, a noxious smell), it would be necessary to evaluate whether the interference was unreasonable in the circumstances. What is reasonable would depend, *inter alia*, on the locality of the plaintiff (inhabitants of industrial areas must expect more interference),[25] the extent of the interference (even in industrial areas, there are limits), and the time of day (a continuous loud noise made during the middle of the night is considered less acceptable than the same during the day).[26]

Nuisance law thus provided a land-use planning, or 'zoning', function,[27] dictating where activities with certain kinds of consequences may or may not take place.[28] By establishing clear and

---

24   *Fletcher* v. *Rylands* (1868), p. 279.

25   *Bliss* v. *Hale* (1838); *Sturges* v. *Bridgeman* (1879).

26   *R.* v. *Neville* (1791); *Colls* v. *Home and Colonial Stores* (1865).

27   See *Colls* v. *Home and Colonial Stores* (1865): 'a dweller in towns cannot be expected to have as pure air, as free from smoke, smell, and noise as if he lived in the country, and distant from other dwellings, and yet an excess of smoke, smell and noise may give a cause of action, but in each case it becomes a matter of degree'.

28   Coase (1960) points out that the two parties would have been free to bargain around this judgment – the doctor selling his right to peaceful enjoyment of his property to the sweet manufacturer – if they so wished. This point is important

readily enforceable property rights in this way, nuisance law enabled parties to strike the balance between environmental amenities and cost. People buying a property in the West End knew that they had a right to be free from air pollution, noise and other interferences. People buying property in Bermondsey knew that they would not be able to take an action against a marginal polluter who was not causing physical damage to property. The differences in property prices in these districts no doubt reflected the differences in amenities.

Nuisance law also contains an efficiency aspect. In areas where nuisance-type interferences are rare, as in much of the British countryside, it is more efficient to grant injunctions against those who cause a nuisance, since the transaction costs of bargaining will be relatively low. By contrast, in areas such as historic Bermondsey, where there were many parties causing nuisance-type interferences, the imposition of an injunction against one party seems iniquitous, yet the imposition of an injunction against all would cause great problems. The transaction costs of bargaining would be very high and if, as a result, many firms were to close, the costs to the local people could be great.[29] Moreover, as a neighbourhood becomes less industrial,

---

but, nevertheless, if such a bargain were struck it would not have affected the general right, as a resident of the West End of London, to be free from the noise of pestles and mortars, so the planning function of the law would remain. (Although, presumably, a point would come when so many defendants had bargained around their respective injunctions that the character of the area would have changed.)

29 If many firms were faced with injunctions, they would have to bargain with each of the affected parties, which might be time consuming and expensive – and most likely some parties would simply refuse any compensation. In the absence of low-cost abatement technologies, the only alternative for many firms might be to move the plant elsewhere.

judges may look more favourably on claims that an individual source of noise or noxious emission constitutes a nuisance. In this context, the English principle that coming to a nuisance is no defence, so clearly propounded in *Sturges* v. *Bridgeman*, helps those seeking to improve the environmental amenities in an area that was formerly industrial.[30]

Finally, the establishment of property rights through decentralised private nuisance actions is, arguably, both more equitable and more efficient than the creation of rights through a system of administrative planning. In the latter system, state administrators decide a priori where industry can locate and bargaining cannot take place, because rights created by administrative planning are inalienable.

Addressing the multiple-source problem

It is often asserted that private law solutions such as nuisance are interesting at an academic level but irrelevant at a practical level because of the problem of multiple sources. This is contradicted, however, by what happened in the St Helen's region. When *St Helen's* v. *Tipping* is discussed, writers rarely mention that the copper smelting company was only one of several companies causing pollution in the area, including an alkali manufacturer. Yet the judges were perfectly aware of this; indeed, it underpinned their decision to separate the tort of nuisance. And they made very

---

30   Another option for improving the environment in an area 'zoned' for industrial use would be for those affected by the pollution to bargain with the companies. The coordination costs of such an activity might, however, be high. Moreover, the bargaining power of those so affected would probably be weak since the very nature of places that are 'zoned' for industrial use implies that the residents are poor.

clear that where physical damage is done to property by an identifiable party, damages will be payable.

The St Helen's experience also contradicts the claim that private law cannot resolve problems when there are multiple plaintiffs. Following the *St Helen's* v. *Tipping* decision, farmers living around St Helen's were able to obtain compensation from the smelting company. Indeed, they were able to do so en masse, through William Rothwell, a land agent and valuer in St Helen's, who acted as arbitrator between the St Helen's Smelting Company and numerous farmers who were adversely affected.[31]

Finally, the St Helen's case demolishes the argument that private law solutions are too lenient on polluters. In 1865, Mr Tipping won an injunction against the smelting company, which led to the closure of the plant and no doubt put the various affected parties on a surer footing to bargain with the alkali works.[32]

Public protection of the environment

A similar situation arose in the context of water pollution, following the case of *Young & Co.* v. *Bankier Distillery Co.* in 1893,[33] which established that riparian owners should have a right to an undiminished flow of water of undiminished quality. As Lord Macnaghten put it in *Young*:

> A riparian owner is entitled to have the water of the
> stream, on the bank of which his property lies, flow down
> as it has been accustomed to flow down to his property,
> subject to the ordinary use of the flowing water by upper

---

31   House of Lords Select Committee on Noxious Vapours (1862).
32   *Tipping* v. *St Helen's*, Eng. Rep. (1865).
33   *Young & Co.* v. *Bankier Distillery Co.* (1893).

> proprietors, and to such further use, if any, on their part in
> connection with the property as may be reasonable in the
> circumstances. Every riparian owner is thus entitled to the
> water of his stream, in its natural flow, without sensible
> diminution or increase, and without sensible alteration in
> its character or quality.[34]

This right enabled riparian owners successfully to sue polluters. Moreover, once the owners had established their rights, they were able typically to bargain with polluters rather than go to court. In some cases, riparian owners forced polluters to stop or to reduce emissions; in other cases they sold some or all of their rights. In each case, however, they achieved the balance of environmental amenities and other goods that best satisfied their subjective preferences.

Riparian rights have also been used to achieve broader goals by a group of conservationists. In 1958, a lawyer who was also a keen angler established an organisation called the Anglers Cooperative Association, in order to improve the quality of Britain's rivers and streams. Anglers have a strong interest in ensuring that waterways are clean because fish are particularly susceptible to certain kinds of water impurities. The ACA indemnifies riparian owners against the cost of bringing a legal action and directly provides the legal services, effectively stepping into the shoes of the riparian owners. The riparian owners thus benefit from these services at minimal cost.[35]

In the nearly 50 years since it was established, the ACA has initiated over 2,000 proceedings against polluters. Nearly all these were settled out of court in favour of the ACA. Where cases have

---

34   Ibid., per Lord Macnaghten.
35   For a fuller discussion of the role of the ACA, see Bate (2001).

come to trial, the ACA has lost on very few occasions. As a result of the actions of the ACA – as well as riparian owners acting independently – Britain's rivers and streams are now almost certainly far cleaner than they would have been had the anglers relied solely upon government regulation.

While the direct beneficiaries have been the riparian owners and the anglers, there are also indirect beneficiaries. These include all those who value clean water and healthier aquatic environments (for the services they provide to other parts of the ecosystem, including the many species of aquatic life that inhabit those streams and rivers).

Economists (and, increasingly, environmentalists) often claim that the state must step in to provide, or subsidise the provision of, certain services on the grounds that the market will not provide those services when market participants can 'free-ride' – that is to say, they cannot be excluded from benefiting and so can obtain the benefits without incurring most of the cost. The actions of the ACA show that where exclusive rights do exists, the legal owners may cooperate with other beneficiaries in a way that substantially reduces – and possibly eliminates – this free-rider problem. Indeed, it is quite plausible that the amount of aquatic life supplied by the ACA actually equals the total amount that would be demanded by all those willing to pay. This is because non-ACA members benefit from *the same* fish and other aquatic species that are conserved by the ACA's actions.

Meanwhile, because successive British governments – and the EU – have seen fit to regulate water quality, it is quite possible that the quality of water in Britain's streams and rivers is *too high*. On the other hand, it may be that government regulation has crowded out contributions to the ACA that would have enabled it to take a greater number of actions and that as a result the quality of water in Britain's streams and rivers is *too low*. Moreover, some water polluters and abstractors have been able to continue engaging in their activities in spite of causing harm to riparian owners because they have been granted statutory authority to do so (by an act of Parliament). Of course, we cannot know whether aquatic life in Britain is under- or over-supplied because there are no reliable ways of measuring people's willingness to pay for these services other than market transactions. What we can know is that government regulation has prevented the 'optimum' quality of water from being achieved.

Conclusion

From the above, we can see how private nuisance law can be an effective means of enabling individuals to satisfy their subjective preferences for environmental quality: if these rules were applied generally, pollution would be limited to areas where people are willing to accept it voluntarily – either because they have purchased a property in an already polluted area (which has become polluted because residents chose not to take an action), or because they have accepted the compensation offered by the polluter.

Unfortunately, since the late eighteenth century nuisance law has been in ever increasing flux and has in many respects been replaced by the law of negligence. Negligence can be found only if a specific 'duty of care' has been breached, which in turn requires that specific duties of care be identified. By contrast, nuisance was traditionally a strict liability tort; that is to say, it would not matter whether the person causing the nuisance had taken all reasonable

THE NEW RURAL ECONOMY

measures to prevent a harm; they would still be liable if the harm were deemed in principle to be actionable. This may seem harsh, but it overcomes the absurdity of attempting after the fact to define what might or might not have been foreseeable prior to an incident and it creates clear 'rules of the game' for all parties.

A return to a more traditional nuisance law would improve its utility as a means of addressing environmental problems, offering at least a partial solution to the conundrum posed in the introduction.

One simple corrective would be for the courts to accept Lord Denning's proposition that statutory authority not override basic common-law rights of action:

> I venture to suggest that modern statutes should be construed on a new principle. Wherever private undertakers seek statutory authority to construct and operate an installation which may cause damage to people living in the neighbourhood, it should not be assumed that Parliament intended that damage should be done to innocent people without redress. Just as in principle property should not be taken compulsorily except on proper compensation being paid for it so, also, in principle property should not be damaged compulsorily except on proper compensation being made for the damage done.[36]

Another corrective would be for courts to reject the ambiguous and uncertain precepts of negligence that today limit the utility of nuisance law, as Lord Denning likewise suggested:

> No matter whether the undertakers use due diligence or not, they ought not to be allowed – for their own profit

---

36   *Allen* v. *Gulf Oil Refining Ltd* (1980), per Lord Denning.

– to damage innocent people or property without paying
compensation. They ought to provide for it as part of the
legitimate expenses of their operation, either as initial
capital cost or the subsequent revenue.[37]

If nuisance and related common-law actions were thereby
permitted a more substantial role in environmental protection,
environmental organisations might follow the ACA model and
indemnify parties who seek to sue polluters, rather than push for
more stringent environmental regulation. Indeed, there might
be a move to repeal the entire body of environmental legislation,
which would soon begin to look cumbersome, expensive and
counter-productive.[38] If the state were to announce in advance
its plans to repeal these regulations, it would signal to the private
sector that a niche is available to be fulfilled and one might expect
a flurry of environmental entrepreneurs to emerge to take up the
slack.

A switch away from command-and-control style environmental regulation and towards a common-law approach would
better enable people to realise their own personal visions for the
environment of the British countryside, whether through individual action or by cooperating with others in groups such as the
ACA. Not all the results would be to the liking of everyone. That
is the nature of individual choice and of experimentation. But it
is difficult to imagine that the situation would be worse than it
is today – with environmental choices determined, as they are,

---

37 Ibid.
38 *Cf.* Cutting (2001) (if property rights advocates truly acknowledged the responsi-
    bilities and the rights of property owners, the remainder of the body of environ-
    mental law as we know it might actually become unnecessary).

largely by unelected bureaucrats implementing the demented visions of central planners.

The main losers from such a shift would be those who seek to impose their vision on others and are able, through the political process, to do so. For those of us who are happy pursuing our own vision of the good life – to the extent that we are able within our narrow sphere of action – things will be a whole lot better. No longer will we have to justify to a busybody from the local authority our nearly every decision to make minor alterations to our house, or to chop down a tree, or to install a pond in our garden. And if as a result of our actions we harm our neighbours' property or their enjoyment thereof, causing for example an unpleasant stink or irritating noise, we will no longer be able to argue in our defence that we are complying with an environmental standard or that we have taken all due care to ensure that no harm arises: we will either have to stop the offending act and pay compensation or we will have to negotiate an agreement with our neighbour.

References

Aldred's Case, 77 Eng. Rep. 816 (KB 1611).

Allen v. *Gulf Oil Refining Ltd* (1980), QB 156.

Bate, R. (2001), *Saving Our Streams*, London: Institute of Economic Affairs.

Baumol, W. J. and W. E. Oates (1988), *The Theory of Environmental Policy*, Cambridge: Cambridge University Press.

Blackstone, W. (n.d.), *Commentaries on the Laws of England*, 3.

Bliss v. *Hale* (1838), 7 LJR 122 (1838).

Brenner, J. F. (1973), 'Nuisance law and the Industrial Revolution', *Journal of Legal Studies*, 3, 2: 403–433.

Calabresi, G. and A. D. Melamed (1972), 'Property rules, liability rules and inalienability: one view of the cathedral', *Harvard Law Review*, 85: 1089–1128.

Cheung, S. (1978), *The Myth of Social Cost*, London: Institute of Economic Affairs.

Coase, R. (1960), 'The problem of social cost', *Journal of Law and Economics*, 3: 1–44.

Colls v. *Home and Colonial Stores* (1865), AC 179.

Coquillette, D. R. (1979), 'Mosses from an old manse: another look at some historic property cases about the environment', *Cornell Law Review*, 64: 761–821.

Coursey, D. L. (1997), 'The revealed demand for a public good: evidence from endangered and threatened species', *New York University Environmental Law Journal*, 6: 411–50.

Cutting, R. (2001), 'One man's ceilin' is another man's floor: property rights as the double edged sword', *Environmental Law*, 31, 4: 819–900.

Ellickson, R. (1973), 'Alternatives to zoning: covenants, nuisance rules and fines as land use controls', *University of Chicago Law Review*, 40, 4: 681–781.

Fletcher v. *Rylands*, 11 Eng. Rep. (1866) LR 1-Ex. 265 (Blackburn), aff'd 3 LR 3 HL 330 (1868).

Hayek, F. A. (1945), 'The use of knowledge in society', *American Economic Review*, 35: 519–30.

House of Lords Select Committee on Noxious Vapours (1862), 'Parliamentary papers', *Minutes of Evidence*, London (21 QQ 220–22).

Jones v. *Powell*, 123 Eng. Rep. 1155 (CP 1628).

Kahneman, D. and J. L. Knetch (1992), 'Valuing public goods: the purchase of moral satisfaction', *Journal of Environmental Economics and Management*, 22: 57–70.

Littlechild, S. C. (1979), 'The problem of social cost', in L. Spardo (ed.), *New Directions in Austrian Economics*, pp. 77–93.

Macaulay, H. H. (1991), 'Liability and environmental quality', in R. E. Meiners and B. Yandle (eds), *The Economic Consequences of Liability Rules*, Westport, CT: Quorum Books.

McLaren, J. P. S. (1983), 'Nuisance law and the Industrial Revolution – some lessons from social history', *Oxford Journal of Legal Studies*, 3, 2: 155–221.

Meiners, R. E. and B. Yandle (eds), *The Economic Consequences of Liability Rules*, Westport, CT: Quorum Books.

Morley v. *Pragnel*, 79 Eng. Rep. 1039 (KB 1638).

Ogus, A. I. and G. M. Richardson (1977), 'Economics and the environment: a study of private nuisance', *Cambridge Law Journal*, 36,2: 284–325.

Pennington, M. (2002), *Liberating the Land*, London: Institute of Economic Affairs.

R. v. *Neville*, 170 Eng. Rep. 102 (1791).

Sagoff, M. (1994), 'Four dogmas of environmental economics', *Environmental Values*, 3: 285–310.

Sturges v. *Bridgeman*, 11 Eng. Rep. 852 (Ch. D. 1879).

Tennant v. *Goldwin*, 92 Eng. Rep. 222 (KB 1705).

Tipping v. *St Helen's*, 11 Eng. Rep. 1483 (HL 1865).

Tuberville v. *Stam*, 88 Eng. Rep. 1228 (KB 1697).

Yandle, B. (1997), *Common Sense and Common Law for the Environment*, Lanham, MD: Rowman & Littlefield.

Young & Co. v. *Bankier Distillery Co.* (1893), AC 698.

ABOUT THE IEA

The Institute is a research and educational charity (No. CC 235 351), limited by guarantee. Its mission is to improve understanding of the fundamental institutions of a free society with particular reference to the role of markets in solving economic and social problems.

The IEA achieves its mission by:

- a high-quality publishing programme
- conferences, seminars, lectures and other events
- outreach to school and college students
- brokering media introductions and appearances

The IEA, which was established in 1955 by the late Sir Antony Fisher, is an educational charity, not a political organisation. It is independent of any political party or group and does not carry on activities intended to affect support for any political party or candidate in any election or referendum, or at any other time. It is financed by sales of publications, conference fees and voluntary donations.

In addition to its main series of publications the IEA also publishes a quarterly journal, *Economic Affairs*.

The IEA is aided in its work by a distinguished international Academic Advisory Council and an eminent panel of Honorary Fellows. Together with other academics, they review prospective IEA publications, their comments being passed on anonymously to authors. All IEA papers are therefore subject to the same rigorous independent refereeing process as used by leading academic journals.

IEA publications enjoy widespread classroom use and course adoptions in schools and universities. They are also sold throughout the world and often translated/reprinted.

Since 1974 the IEA has helped to create a world-wide network of 100 similar institutions in over 70 countries. They are all independent but share the IEA's mission.

Views expressed in the IEA's publications are those of the authors, not those of the Institute (which has no corporate view), its Managing Trustees, Academic Advisory Council members or senior staff.

Members of the Institute's Academic Advisory Council, Honorary Fellows, Trustees and Staff are listed on the following page.

The Institute gratefully acknowledges financial support for its publications programme and other work from a generous benefaction by the late Alec and Beryl Warren.

Other papers recently published by the IEA include:

WHO, What and Why?

Transnational Government, Legitimacy and the World Health Organization
Roger Scruton
Occasional Paper 113; ISBN 0 255 36487 3
£8.00

The World Turned Rightside Up

A New Trading Agenda for the Age of Globalisation
John C. Hulsman
Occasional Paper 114; ISBN 0 255 36495 4
£8.00

The Representation of Business in English Literature

Introduced and edited by Arthur Pollard
Readings 53; ISBN 0 255 36491 1
£12.00

Anti-Liberalism 2000

The Rise of New Millennium Collectivism
David Henderson
Occasional Paper 115; ISBN 0 255 36497 0
£7.50

Capitalism, Morality and Markets

Brian Griffiths, Robert A. Sirico, Norman Barry & Frank Field
Readings 54; ISBN 0 255 36496 2
£7.50

Saving Our Streams

The Role of the Anglers' Conservation Association in
Protecting English and Welsh Rivers
Roger Bate
Research Monograph 53; ISBN 0 255 36494 6
£10.00

Better Off Out?

The Benefits or Costs of EU Membership
Brian Hindley & Martin Howe
Occasional Paper 99 (new edition); ISBN 0 255 36502 0
£10.00

Buckingham at 25

Freeing the Universities from State Control
Edited by James Tooley
Readings 55; ISBN 0 255 36512 8
£15.00

Lectures on Regulatory and Competition Policy

Irwin M. Stelzer
Occasional Paper 120; ISBN 0 255 36511 X
£12.50

Misguided Virtue

False Notions of Corporate Social Responsibility
David Henderson
Hobart Paper 142; ISBN 0 255 36510 1
£12.50

HIV and Aids in Schools

The Political Economy of Pressure Groups and Miseducation
Barrie Craven, Pauline Dixon, Gordon Stewart & James Tooley
Occasional Paper 121; ISBN 0 255 36522 5
£10.00

The Road to Serfdom

The Reader's Digest *condensed version*
Friedrich A. Hayek
Occasional Paper 122; ISBN 0 255 36530 6
£7.50

Bastiat's *The Law*

Introduction by Norman Barry
Occasional Paper 123; ISBN 0 255 36509 8
£7.50

A Globalist Manifesto for Public Policy

Charles Calomiris
Occasional Paper 124; ISBN 0 255 36525 x
£7.50

Euthanasia for Death Duties

Putting Inheritance Tax Out of Its Misery
Barry Bracewell-Milnes
Research Monograph 54; ISBN 0 255 36513 6
£10.00

Liberating the Land

The Case for Private Land-use Planning
Mark Pennington
Hobart Paper 143; ISBN 0 255 36508 x
£10.00

IEA Yearbook of Government Performance 2002/2003

Edited by Peter Warburton
Yearbook 1; ISBN 0 255 36532 2
£15.00

Britain's Relative Economic Performance, 1870–1999

Nicholas Crafts
Research Monograph 55; ISBN 0 255 36524 1
£10.00

Should We Have Faith in Central Banks?

Otmar Issing
Occasional Paper 125; ISBN 0 255 36528 4
£7.50

The Dilemma of Democracy

Arthur Seldon
Hobart Paper 136 (reissue); ISBN 0 255 36536 5
£10.00

Capital Controls: a 'Cure' Worse Than the Problem?
Forrest Capie
Research Monograph 56; ISBN 0 255 36506 3
£10.00

The Poverty of 'Development Economics'
Deepak Lal
Hobart Paper 144 (reissue); ISBN 0 255 36519 5
£15.00

Should Britain Join the Euro?
The Chancellor's Five Tests Examined
Patrick Minford
Occasional Paper 126; ISBN 0 255 36527 6
£7.50

Post-Communist Transition: Some Lessons
Leszek Balcerowicz
Occasional Paper 127; ISBN 0 255 36533 0
£7.50

A Tribute to Peter Bauer
John Blundell et al.
Occasional Paper 128; ISBN 0 255 36531 4
£10.00

Employment Tribunals
Their Growth and the Case for Radical Reform
J. R. Shackleton
Hobart Paper 145; ISBN 0 255 36515 2
£10.00

Fifty Economic Fallacies Exposed
Geoffrey E. Wood
Occasional Paper 129; ISBN 0 255 36518 7
£12.50

A Market in Airport Slots
Keith Boyfield (editor), David Starkie, Tom Bass & Barry Humphreys
Readings 56; ISBN 0 255 36505 5
£10.00

Money, Inflation and the Constitutional Position of the Central Bank
Milton Friedman & Charles A. E. Goodhart
Readings 57; ISBN 0 255 36538 1
£10.00

railway.com
Parallels between the Early British Railways and the ICT Revolution
Robert C. B. Miller
Research Monograph 57; ISBN 0 255 36534 9
£12.50

The Regulation of Financial Markets
Edited by Philip Booth & David Currie
Readings 58; ISBN 0 255 36551 9
£12.50

Climate Alarmism Reconsidered
Robert L. Bradley Jr
Hobart Paper 146; ISBN 0 255 36541 1
£12.50

Government Failure: E. G. West on Education
Edited by James Tooley & James Stanfield
Occasional Paper 130; ISBN 0 255 36552 7
£12.50

Waging the War of Ideas
John Blundell
Second edition
Occasional Paper 131; ISBN 0 255 36547 0
£12.50

Corporate Governance: Accountability in the Marketplace
Elaine Sternberg
Second edition
Hobart Paper 147; ISBN 0 255 36542 X
£12.50

The Land Use Planning System
Evaluating Options for Reform
John Corkindale
Hobart Paper 148; ISBN 0 255 36550 0
£10.00

The Role of Business in the Modern World
Progress, Pressures, and Prospects for the Market Economy
David Henderson
Hobart Paper 150; ISBN 0 255 36548 9
£12.50

Public Service Broadcasting Without the BBC?
Alan Peacock
Occasional Paper 133; ISBN 0 255 36565 9
£10.00

The ECB and the Euro: the First Five Years
Otmar Issing
Occasional Paper 134; ISBN 0 255 36555 1
£10.00

Towards a Liberal Utopia?
Edited by Philip Booth
Hobart Paperback 32; ISBN 0 255 36563 2
£15.00

The Way Out of the Pensions Quagmire
Philip Booth & Deborah Cooper
Research Monograph 60; ISBN 0 255 36517 9
£12.50

Black Wednesday
A Re-examination of Britain's Experience in the Exchange Rate Mechanism
Alan Budd
Occasional Paper 135; ISBN 0 255 36566 7
£7.50

Crime: Economic Incentives and Social Networks
Paul Ormerod
Hobart Paper 151; ISBN 0 255 36554 3
£10.00

The Road to Serfdom *with* The Intellectuals and Socialism
Friedrich A. Hayek
Occasional Paper 136; ISBN 0 255 36576 4
£10.00

Money and Asset Prices in Boom and Bust
Tim Congdon
Hobart Paper 152; ISBN 0 255 36570 5
£10.00

Money and Asset Prices in Boom and Bust
Tim Congdon
Hobart Paper 152; ISBN 0 255 36570 5
£10.00

The Dangers of Bus Re-regulation
and Other Perspectives on Markets in Transport
John Hibbs et al.
Occasional Paper 137; ISBN 0 255 36572 1
£10.00

To order copies of currently available IEA papers, or to enquire about availability, please contact:

Lavis Marketing
IEA orders
FREEPOST LON21280
Oxford OX3 7BR

Tel: 01865 767575
Fax: 01865 750079
Email: orders@lavismarketing.co.uk

The IEA also offers a subscription service to its publications. For a single annual payment, currently £40.00 in the UK, you will receive every monograph the IEA publishes during the course of a year and discounts on our extensive back catalogue. For more information, please contact:

Adam Myers
Subscriptions
The Institute of Economic Affairs
2 Lord North Street
London SW1P 3LB

Tel: 020 7799 8920
Fax: 020 7799 2137
Website: www.iea.org.uk